The Genesis of Language

THE FIRST MICHIGAN COLLOQUIUM
1979

The Genesis of Language

Edited by Kenneth C. Hill

1979
KAROMA PUBLISHERS, INC.　　ANN ARBOR

IN MEMORIAM: DAVID DECAMP

ISBN: 0-89720-024-1 (Cloth); 0-89720-025-X (Paper)

Printed in the United States of America

CONTENTS

INTRODUCTION
Kenneth C. Hill

Each year the Department of Linguistics receives a modest sum of money from the College as a lecture fund. Usually speakers are invited quite independently of each other; they come, they give their talks, we pass a pleasant time with them, and that's that. Those who attend a lecture often get something of considerable value from the experience, but the overall impact of such lectures is necessarily rather limited. This year we decided to use our lecture money a little differently, so there would be a more long-lasting contribution. We would invite a series of speakers—all to talk on the same topic. Each lecture would be recorded so that each speaker would know precisely what had been said by previous speakers; and each speaker would know that subsequent speakers would hear him or her, that each subsequent speaker was, in effect, in the audience. We sent the recordings to the speakers well in advance of their coming to Ann Arbor. The result was something like a year-long conference. And we would publish the presentations in a timely way so that linguists at large could share in the immediacy of our experience. Hence, this volume.

The topic we decided on for our series this year was the "genesis of language," with particular focus on pidgins and creoles as a special sort of laboratory for investigating and understanding language genesis. I believe this topic occurred to us initially simply because of the availability of Derek Bickerton as a speaker; he was on sabbatical leave from Hawaii, and we could afford to bring him to Ann Arbor. Once we had thought of it, this topic struck us as particularly appropriate for this first series. It represents a continuity with the theme of the 1973 Linguistic Institute held at the University of Michigan (two of our speakers, Bickerton and Sankoff, were participants in that Institute), and it has come to be a lively topic in the field generally. This is attested by the success of the recent conference on creoles on St. Thomas (Conference on Theoretical Orientations in Creole Studies, March 28 through April 1, 1979) and by the fact that the Linguistic Society of America is planning a special symposium on second language acquisition and pidgins and creoles for its upcoming 1979 winter meeting.

It is interesting how so often concerns that are peripheral at one point in a field's history become central at another point. Early students of pidgins and creoles were for years consigned to oblivion or near-oblivion within linguistics, probably largely because their subject matter seemed to be just those sorts of languages which did not show orderly development, and the investigation of the orderliness of the historical development was the principal mission and great triumph of 19th-century and early 20th-century linguistics. An example of such a once-forgotten scholar is Hesseling (see Muysken and Meijer's Introduction to Hesseling 1979). More famous is Hugo Schuchardt, who questioned the universal applicability of sound laws; only now is Schuchardt's work being translated into English (1979), now that advances in creole studies have provided us with a context in which we can appreciate this work. Of course the explication of orderliness in language really is the mission of linguistics, and major advances in linguistics align with discoveries of how wider and wider ranges of linguistic behavior are amenable to orderly description. Pidgins and creoles are now seen to have orderliness in their historical development, but an orderliness of a rather special sort—one which suggests to some observers the workings of deep psycholinguistic and language-universal processes, and one often more amenable to analysis in terms of gradience instead of contrast. Other observers, also recognizing the nonchaotic nature of the development of pidgins and creoles, find their explanations in rather more language-specific data. Herein lies active controversy, and we hoped to build our series around it.

Not only have pidgin and creole studies provided a new arena for the testing of theories of universals of language acquisition, and in their spectacular variation a new context for the application of analysis in terms of gradience and wave theory, but also they have been a principal arena for the revival of functionalism, long denigrated in linguistics. Bickerton's hypotheses in the present volume about the relationship of pidgin and creole development to the context of plantation society are an excellent example of the revival of functionalism. The work of Sankoff and her colleagues on syntactic developments in Tok Pisin as its speakers move it into new functional contexts is another example of a type of analysis which has awakened renewed interest in functional analysis and attention to the "external factors" in language change, which have for a long time been all too peripheral in historical linguistic scholarship.

Few of us appreciated, in planning the 1973 Linguistic Institute, how visionary William Labov was when, as Associate Director of the Institute, he insisted that studying language in context entails studying pidgins and creoles, and he made sure we included creolists among the visiting faculty. These scholars were then, to be sure, even just six years ago, considerably less well known than they are today.

Choosing our contributors was, in retrospect, rather straightforward. We were already starting off with Bickerton. He and Gillian Sankoff were the creolists on the visiting faculty for the 1973 Institute, and as Bickerton and Sankoff find themselves on opposite sides of a rather important theoretical issue, Sankoff was an obvious choice to follow Bickerton. (Bickerton's view is that some important qualitative changes occur as a pidgin becomes a creole, that is, acquires native speakers; Sankoff holds that a pidgin is enough: under the right circumstances a language even in the absence of native speakers undergoes the qualitative changes at issue.) John Schumann was a clear choice to give a second language perspective, and Mervyn Alleyne, with his claim that the Atlantic creoles owe much of their structure to the contribution of African languages, provides us with a good counterbalance to the strong innatist and universalist stance of the other speakers. Rodney Moag happened to be visiting here teaching Hindi during Peter Hook's absence in India this year, and, as he had just completed a stint in Fiji working with, among other things, Fiji-Pidgin-Hindi and Hindi-Pidgin-Fiji, it seemed only right to ask him to participate in the series. We weren't able to have Ellen Woolford and William Washabaugh come as speakers, but it is with great pleasure that we are able to include their contributions.

Of course many perspectives have had to be excluded. I wish we had been able to include someone to speak on creoles from more of an anthropological perspective, with attention to the social conditions under which creoles originated, and I thought the "genesis of language" ought to have included something having to do with language origins in remotest prehistory, especially as that subject has recently become respectable again. Others may miss the very data-oriented and carefully documented sort of work associated with Labov and his colleagues, and considerably emphasized here in the 1973 Institute. But we couldn't tell our speakers what to say—and we wanted them to be spontaneous and to talk about what they were thinking right now—and we could invite only a few speakers. And we could never hope to touch on all facets of language genesis anyway.

What success our series has had this year is due to the efforts of a number of people, outstanding among whom has to be Thomas Markey, who participated throughout in the planning and organizing, and who made many of the initial contacts with the speakers. Without his efforts we would not have gotten started on this at all, and would not now be planning another series for next year. We also owe a great deal to the efforts of Sandra Fine, the Administrative Assistant in the Department of Linguistics. We must thank Frank Casa, Chairman of the Department of Romance Languages and Literatures. Part way along the line we discovered that we had over-committed our funds, and Casa helped us out of a potential embarrassment by committing what was left at that time of his department's lecture funds. Even that wasn't enough, and we would like to acknowledge here the contri-bution of the anonymous benefactor(s) of the Linguistics Department Special Fund, which made up the difference in the end.

Thus we are sharing with you these presentations and commentary, which show how a number of leading scholars in the field are thinking right now. Some of these contributions are rather informal, but none lacks spontaneity, which in this volatile subject may be most valuable. Unfortunately, we can't share with you the warmth of the personal interactions which we have en-joyed so, the memories of late evening conversations and red wine.

Kenneth C. Hill
Ann Arbor
July 1979

BEGINNINGS
Derek Bickerton

I've taken my coat off. It doesn't mean I want to fight any-body—quite the reverse, I want to say how nice it is to be back here. I was here as some of you may remember for the summer Linguistic Institute of 1973 and haven't been back since, but it still is great to be here and see all those familiar faces.

The Genesis of Language

There are not many languages about which we can even start to think in terms of genesis, on account of these things tend to be lost in the midst of ancient history. And if we're going to ask ourselves about the genesis of English, the genesis of Swahili, the genesis of any language you can think of, we're going to go back into very considerable time depth. When you start to ask about the genesis of creole languages, however, you're dealing with a time depth which is maximum four or five hundred years. And you might think that on the face of things it would be relatively easy to find facts about the genesis of these languages which are so recent in time. But it turns out to be just as difficult.

What is striking about creole languages is that contrary to other languages we can approximately date their birth. We can say that for instance before 1650 there was no Sranan. The language simply did not exist, the area where it was going to be spoken simply was not populated. What happens with these languages is that first of all a pidgin language originates. And in most of the cases, it originated through a plantation culture being established in one of these areas. Large numbers of people were brought from different parts of the world speaking languages which were not mutually intelligible, and therefore people in this situation were forced to create some kind of functional con-tact language that would enable them to talk to one another.

Well, fair enough, but what happened straight after that was that children were born to these people, and I'm going to go into a little more detail on what it meant to be a child in a pidgin-speaking community in a little while. What happened in very crude terms was that children would grow up in a society which was a pidgin-speaking society. They would take a pidgin language and "develop" it so that it became an adequate vehicle for all they had to express about their needs, their wants or their desires which the pidgin language that preceded them could not have done. And it is this expansion I want to talk about today. What do we mean when we say a pidgin language expands and becomes a creole language?

I'll go back for a little bit historically just to look at a few of the things that have been said about creole languages. Creole languages first of all were regarded simply as corrupted forms of European languages. Most of them in fact were attached to European languages in some sense; they sprang up as a result of European colonialism. Their vocabularies were largely composed of European lexical items, and it was very easy for people in the 19th century to look at these languages and to say, "Well," given the ideas that were current at the time, "Well, you know, it's obvious these poor, uneducated lower orders of people are just not equipped to learn the profound subtleties of French," or English, or whatever.

So naturally these languages came out kind of weird and were regarded as broken languages, the result of pure intellectual incapacity. This idea I suppose prevailed in lay circles for a long time. It wasn't until toward the end of the 19th century that Schuchardt became interested in these languages largely because of his long fight with the neogrammarians. He was opposed to the idea that a new language could only come about through some kind of Stammbaum process, some kind of genetic tree so that every language has but one parent, in contradistinction to every other kind of living organism. In Schuchardt's view a language could have two parents like everything else. There could have been maybe an Indo-European parent on the one hand and maybe an African or Asian or whatever parent on the other. Thus, he was largely concerned with proving that you could have mixed languages—which of course was one of the controversies of that period: whether or not it was possible to have a mixed language; according to the neogrammarians you could not have. Schuchardt was less interested in specifically what the mixture consisted of. But later, people began to look at these mixtures, and the first approximation to saying what you could mix was fairly simplistic, as represented by writers like Suzanne Sylvain who wrote about Haitian Creole and who claimed that Haitian Creole was a kind of merger of French lexicon and the syntax of Ewe, which is one of the Kwa group of languages on the coast of West Africa. So, this involves supposing that you could take language components—a lexicon from one language, a syntax from another—slap them together and get a third language. Again, this is a little too simplistic, as people found out when they began to compare a little more closely the syntaxes of these languages with the syntaxes of some of the substratum languages involved. I know this from personal experience because I did a lot of this around 1971 when I was interested to see if there were any possibility of tracing the verbal system of Guyanese Creole back to some kind of West African ancestor.

What happens is that the closer you look at African grammars, the more you see how different they are—the incredible range of different types of language even within the Kwa group, let alone within West African languages as a whole. And although there are here and there some sweeping similarities which tease you and provoke you to go on with the search, you never find any language which has quite the same kinds of structures as the creole language does.

What you do find, and this is stage three now in the history of creole linguistics, what you *did* find was that there were also similarities among different creole languages, similarities such that you would not have predicted them for any languages that weren't in some sense genetically related. I'll just give you what were, I suppose, among the most striking of such similarities. Within the verbal system, or system of tense-aspect I should say, each creole language has three, no more and no less than three, tense-aspect markers. And I'm not distinguishing here between tense and aspect—I know there are lots of people who seem to think that they know the difference between these two things, but I've never managed to find it myself, least of all in these languages, where not only facts about time but also facts about the kind of action are conveyed or implied by the same single marker. So, what you have are three categories: one category I call anterior; one category, irrealis; one category, non-punctual. An anterior marker is like the pluperfect but not quite. It would take too long for me to explain exactly how it differs from the pluperfect; it certainly isn't a straight past marker although it is often misanalyzed as such. It's a kind of discourse marker which is used to signal states or events which are anterior to things which have been under discussion in the course of the same discourse. And markers like that, like *bin,* or *en,* or *te,* or *ya,* these will differ from creole to creole. What is striking about the creoles is that no matter if the phonological form of the markers varies—and it does—from one language to another, the semantic area covered by the marker is either identical or close to identical, even when you're dealing with creoles which have quite different linguistic affiliations, or when these creoles are separated by 6,000 miles of ocean; these things seem to make little difference.

Then we come to irrealis markers. We have in Haitian *ava,* and in Sranan *sa;* you have *go* in most of the Anglo creoles; you have *ke* in the small islands, the French Antilles; and you have *lo* in Papiamentu. Again different forms, again with the same broad general area of meaning. And this meaning covers everything that doesn't seem to have really happened, things you might in other languages express in terms of future, subjunctive, conditional; no matter what, they're all expressed in terms of the irrealis marker.

Then, you have non-punctual markers. The non-punctual marker again embraces habitual, iterative, and also continuative and progressive. Any action that is not a point action, a single action at a particular instant of time, would be marked by a non-punctual marker. In Haitian it's *ap; ka* in the lesser Antilles; you have *ta* in the Spanish- or Portuguese-related ones. You can have *de* or *e; e* is the Sranan one derived from the original locative verb *de*. In Guyanese Creole, it is *a;* in Hawaiian, you have *stay.* So, no matter what surface forms you have—and these surface forms are widely different—the semantics of them, the expression of both duration and iteration by the same marker is found.

Not only are these three types of markers present in all creoles, but the order of them, should they co-occur, is always the same. That is to say one, two, three. If you have an anterior marker, it will precede either an irrealis or a non-punctual. If you get an irrealis, it goes before non-punctual. The only exception I know to this is the *lo* of Papiamentu which can occur sentence initially. But I was told by Morris Goodman yesterday in Chicago that you in fact find *lo* in Papiamentu also in this position. So, this is a kind of pidgin hangover in Papiamentu, because one characteristic of pidgin languages as distinct from creole languages—in a moment I will touch briefly on the differences between pidgin languages and creole languages—is that they have tense and aspect markers exterior to the sentence. They're used like sentence adverbials. They occur sentence initially or sentence finally, and Gillian Sankoff had an example of that of course in Tok Pisin *bai,* derived from *baimbai,* originally *bambai* in the pidgin stage of Tok Pisin; it's also an irrealis marker, and it also occurred sentence initially. First thing that happens when Tok Pisin creolizes is that *bai* moves into its regular position at the beginning of the verb phrase.

So, this is just one thing. If I had the time, I could go into other things. Determiner systems are remarkably similar. The movement rules are remarkably similar. Focusing and topicalization are remarkably similar throughout creole languages. Some similarities you wouldn't expect to find unless the languages had a common parent. So, the next step would be to produce a common parent for creoles. And this was done in 1961.

In 1961 Wally Thompson wrote a paper which pointed out these similarities and suggested that there must be a common parent and there must have been some original creole which gave rise to all these forms. A few years later Keith Whinnom wrote an article in which he traced the ancestry of this as far back as the medieval Lingua Franca of the Mediterranean basin—the trading language that was used in the Middle Ages pretty well throughout the Mediterranean.

Now, we have to extend a certain amount of caution toward what he is saying because it taxes the imagination to suppose that a single parent language could have given rise to literally dozens of different languages scattered around the globe, yet which miraculously preserved to an extraordinary degree the same type of syntactic structure that was in their parent. This is not usually the case; normally when languages get as widely diffused as that, changes happen to them. We're being asked to suppose that no matter how far this language was disseminated and no matter how many groups of people it was used among and no matter how different their circumstances were, the basic structure of creole was preserved. And, we're being asked to believe not only that, but that originally this language must have had a predominantly Portuguese lexicon. Because the most plausible explanation—leaving aside the Lingua Franca for the moment—the most plausible explanation is that the original contact language emerged from the Portuguese exploration of West Africa around 1500 and that the Portuguese then disseminated this language to various parts of the globe as far as Macao in China; and subsequently as more and more waves of colonists came out, the language relexified, that is to say that it retained its structure but that it swapped its vocabulary over. There is, as you see, a difficulty in believing in this particular theory—the idea that language cannot merely maintain its syntax intact but that it can drop its Portuguese vocabulary. If it happens to come in contact with French colonialists, it can take on a French vocabulary. If it happens to be overwhelmed by English colonialists, it takes on English vocabulary and so forth. But, in spite of the difficulty of believing in such a theory, it pretty well held the ground, I suppose, certainly through the middle of this decade, because there was no alternative explanation. And as Sherlock Holmes says in one of his adventures, if you eliminate the impossible, what is left, however unlikely, must be true. And I think this is the best and probably the only reason for believing in the theory of monogenesis, or should I say monogenesis plus lexification, for if you believe in one, you've got to believe in the other.

Well, unfortunately, in recent years there have come up some very, very strong arguments against this theory. For instance, in the southern Sudan around the town of Juba there is found a variety of creolized Arabic known as Juba-Arabic which apparently came into existence because of the British

using Arabic-speaking soldiers in their attempt to drive a railroad from the
Cape to Cairo. To do that, they had to conquer all the people in between the
Cape and Cairo, and they didn't get all that far. They kind of got bogged
down in places like the southern Sudan, and the *askaris,* who were Arabic
speakers, settled there and intermarried with predominantly Chadic-speaking
people in and around Juba, and sooner or later, of course, the Arabic which
had been pidginized became creolized because there were now native-born
speakers of Juba-Arabic. And there's an interesting dissertation which should
be available very shortly from Uskari Mahmoud, a Sudanese at Georgetown
University who has written about this language. It's quite clear, from Mahmoud's work, that Juba-Arabic follows the pattern of creoles in things like
the tense markers and in the way in which the tense markers are combined.
I forgot to mention that these tense markers can be combined, and that
their combinations in languages which do combine them yield similar meanings. For instance, a combination of anterior and irrealis is used to express
unrealized conditions in the past, things like "if you had come, I would
have been pleased."

So, there's no possibility that the Portuguese or anyone influenced by
Afro-Portuguese pidgins could ever have had anything to do with the making
of Juba-Arabic. Nobody had ever gone into that area; it was totally unknown
to Europeans or their cohorts until the late 19th century, so that it was
entirely within the Arab sphere of influence. So the theory of monogenesis
will not explain similarities that exist between Juba-Arabic and the other
creoles.

The question that now arises is, what will explain that similarity? I began
to think about this, I guess, around the time of that Summer Institute in
1973, or shortly afterward. And something that seems to have occurred
to me with blinding clarity was that *if* languages *thousands* of miles apart
without any kind of genetic affiliation—languages with different superstrata,
languages with different substrata—if these languages persist in coming out
according to the same pattern, what could be more likely to account for
this than some characteristics that are presumably innate to the human
species? Could it be possible that these similarities in some sense reflected an
innate language faculty? And so I began to work upon this idea and to see
just exactly how far it would take me.

Let's consider, first of all, what the position would be of the creators of
the creole languages? You have to assume that (first of all let's take a paradigm case; I think this is probably the best way to do it) not all creoles are
born in exactly these circumstances, but most of them are born in these

circumstances. These are the circumstances which if somebody said to you, "Go out and start a creole language," you'd be best advised to follow. First of all acquire an island somewhere in the tropics, preferably one that will grow sugar. I don't quite know what the connection between creole and sugar is, I think it's purely accidental, but it's there anyway. The date should be between 1600 and 1750, so throw yourselves back two or three centuries. You're going back two or three centuries, and you're going to make your fortune growing sugar. So, you find an island which hasn't any people on it, or if it has, just a few that you can kill off conveniently. Then, you need a labor force, so you get your labor force. At that time there were lots of people going around in the slave business. And so all you have to do is get hold of a sufficient number of slaves to work your sugar plantation. But you'd be ill advised if you got slaves from the same language group because the first thing they would do once they got there is start putting their heads together and say, "Hey, fellas, we all speak the same language; all we gotta do is, you go this way, I'll go that, and we'll get rid of the slave owner's head and we're in business." So in order to minimize this, plantation owners deliberately recruited slaves from as many different language communities as they could. What you had then was a community of people. You had a small exploitative elite on top of the pile, and underneath you had a large number of people who were brought totally against their wills into this society and who spoke x number of mutually unintelligible languages. We don't know in any case what the original mix was. We do know there was a mix, and we do know that West African languages are quite widely different. So there was obviously a profound communication problem right from the start.

Now, the communication problems of course affect the adults first, and how are they going to cope with that? There's a problem in a situation like this in using any of the existing substratum languages as the base of your contact language. Obviously, if you're an Ewe speaker and someone comes along and says, "Well, look, I think that the language of this plantation will be based on Fanti," you're going to say, "Oh, I'm an Ewe; if you use Fanti, you're putting me at a disadvantage." The advantage of using the superstrate language as a vehicle lay in the fact that it was mutual to everybody. And I think this is something that should be stressed more often than what people normally stress, because what they normally say is this is the language in which the plantation owners and overseers have to give commands. But stop and think a minute: you know you don't need all that much in commands in a tyrannical society of this nature. The amount of linguistic interaction between the bosses and the workers is going to be negligible compared to the interaction of the workers themselves. However, the minimal vocabulary supplied by the overseers is going to be the only thing that everybody has in common. And that's why when they start to build an auxiliary language, they're going to build it mainly out of the lexical building blocks that are provided by the superordinate group. They can derive a lexicon in this way, but they're not going to derive syntactic rules out of the superordinate language for obvious reasons. They don't get sufficient input from the superordinate language to be able to induce the grammatical rules of that language. So they make up the deficiencies by supplying syntactic rules of their own. And in a pidgin you really *can* get the situation where you get the words of language "A," which is the superordinate language, and syntactic structures from languages "X, Y, and Z," which are the subordinate languages. Now, notice that this is not entirely reconstruction either because over the last few years I've been privileged to be in one of the few places in the world where a pidgin language still survives—Hawaii. It survives there for the very simple reason that the Hawaiian pidgin does not date from the first European contact. The first European contact was strictly between English speakers and Hawaiian speakers and produced a language known as *hapa haole* which is quite distinct from the subsequent pidgin. And I can tell you in one sentence how it's distinct from the subsequent pidgin. You take any piece of *hapa haole,* and you can reconstitute it into English by adding the missing morphemes. It's like a kind of game, you know, like a puzzle—reconstitute the *hapa haole* by adding the missing morphemes. But you take a piece of plantation pidgin dating from the post-*hapa haole* period and then put morphemes in there to reconstitute it into English, and there's *no way* you can do it. It's all back to front; no way by simply adding a few grammatical morphemes to it can you make anything that looks even remotely like English. So we have the advantage then that the real pidgin only began, it didn't *even* begin, in 1876. Up until 1876 in Hawaii there were only English and Hawaiian. After the passage of the Sugar Act of 1876 which enabled people to get good prices for their sugar in the U. S., when the sugar industry boomed, then people had to get labor fast. They brought in a rapid succession of Japanese, Chinese, Portuguese, Filipino and large numbers of other smaller groups. But in the first instance, when a pidgin was formed, since the previous plantations founded prior to 1876 had been staffed by Hawaiians and since the language of work, the language of control in these plantations had been Hawaiian, the first pidgin in Hawaii was Pidgin Hawaiian. It even has a name: it is called *olelo hapiai* which means literally 'language of the wet taro' because the first kind of funny Hawaiian that was spoken in Hawaii was spoken by Chinese who were growers of wetland taro. So, this language flourished, unknown to linguistic science entirely, between 1876 and about 1896; and gradually, gradually as Hawaiian began to die and as English became more powerful, Pidgin English took over. So Pidgin English really only dates from the turn of the century.

This means that floating around Hawaii still in their 70's and 80's, but fortunately hale and spry in many cases, are speakers of the earliest Hawaiian Pidgin English. And you can compare the speech of these people with the speech of their children which has of course already become a creole. Now there's a profound difference between these two things. Let's talk for a moment about the pidgin.

You'll find Japanese speakers, people who are immigrants from Japan who may have been in Hawaii at least 50 or more years, and their Pidgin English, even the lexical content of their so-called "Pidgin English," may be 60 or more percent Japanese. Amazing! They really think they're speaking English, but they're not. The sentence structure of these speakers will be 90 percent SOV, and then when you come to look at the Filipino speaker, among Filipino speakers of pidgin you will never find SOV sentences, but you will find VS sentences!! So that what happens then is that the syntax of the pidgin speaker in this early pidgin stage seems to reflect the original syntax of his native language to which has been added a portion of the English lexicon.

So, the one thing that struck me about the pidgin, looking at it in Hawaii, was: what an immense diversity! It differs literally from speaker to speaker. In Hawaii there was never anything that you could call a uniform system. It's possible to identify differences in speakers' nationalities, points of origin, simply by looking at their syntax. It's easier to listen to them of course, but you don't have to listen to them. You can just look at a couple of sentences, and you can tell whether the speaker has a Japanese or Filipino or whatever background. And if this is so, then it occurred to me: how was a child to learn language?

We're told by Chomsky, I think it's in *Aspects,* that the child who's born in a given community has the task of finding out within that community which of the possible human languages it is that is spoken. The child, according to Chomsky, comes into life equipped with a whole set of formal universals. Now formal universals in effect define what theoretically possible languages a human child cannot speak. He cannot speak a language that violates certain strict constraints. He cannot speak a language that violates the complex NP constraint or subjacency, or the specified subject constraint, or whatever those constraints might be. But within that area that's left to him, he can learn any language that falls within the limits imposed upon natural human language, right? Now, what's a child to do? Try to imagine that you are very small, you are about two. You are struggling to go out in the community where a dozen or more languages may be spoken. One of those languages, the superordinate language, you have negligible access to because you're a member of the slave class or the indentured labor class or whatever, so you don't exactly get to hobnob with all those people who ride around occasionally on horses waving whips. You don't get any exposure to their language. How can you learn it if you don't get enough input? So, why don't you learn the language of your mother and father like everybody else does? Of course, you do, when you're starting off, while you're still in the home. You're not in the home very long in cultures like this. We're not talking now about bourgeois Western homes where little Johnny is kept safely tucked up in the nursery until he's about five and then, with traumatic scenes of fear and trembling, mother leads him by the hand and it's the first time he comes in contact with others of his own age. On the contrary, as soon as these guys crawl, they're thrown out into the plantation yard to mix and mingle with whatever other little kids are there. Maybe another sibling is told, "Kinda see that nobody treads on Johnny, if you can."

But that's about as far as it goes. And there's little Johnny in the middle of the yard. And little Johnny, let's say, happened to be brought up by a Japanese mother and father and he goes there hopefully speaking Japanese, or what little two-year-old Japanese he knows. The little boy runs into a two-year-old Chinese, and that freaks him out straightaway, so he crawls along to the next little child and tries him out, and lo and behold! the next little child is Hawaiian. Oh terrible! So he goes on to a third little child; he gets Tagalog. He goes to a fourth little child, and he gets Korean. What's he going to do? He's going to realize that the language of his mother and father is not going to get him any place in the larger society into which he's been so rudely thrust. So he's going to have to learn the pidgin which is the only thing that everybody speaks even though it's grossly inadequate, even though its lento tempo is so gross that listening to a pidgin speaker you often almost go to sleep before he finishes his sentence.

So actually you're amazed by the slowness of some of these speakers, and by the "stripped-downness" of these speakers, because among classic pidgin speakers in Hawaii you will find not just shallow embedding but no embedding at all. You will find no relative clauses, few or no NP complements, that kind of thing. You'll find very, very rudimentary sentence structures, and you'll find virtually no or very little attempt at tense marking at all. Any kind of tense marking that you do find will be completely sporadic. The guy will maybe throw in an occasional "been" if he's taking about the past or an occasional "by and by" if he's talking about the future, but there's absolutely no pattern—most verb phrases consist of just the main stem verb. And how is a child like that to use this truncated, this reduced auxiliary language as his native language? It doesn't matter for parents that the language has been sharply reduced. No matter how small the linguistic groups in any of these situations, there are always enough people in it to constitute a peer group for any individual; he can always make his own personal friends within his own language group, he can always marry into his own language group if he so desires, and he can always carry out most of his social transactions with his own language group. Even if that language group is only a tiny fraction of the social community, he can still exist within it. And all he needs the pidgin for is the times he is forced to go out, the times he's forced to go and buy at the store from some member of some other ethnic group, the times he's forced to talk to his overseer who is a member of some other ethnic group, and so on. He doesn't need much for that, so the pidgin is adequate. But it's not adequate to serve as a native language for anybody at all.

So what happens then is that there is a definite level of complexity that the language has to reach in order to serve as a native tongue. Suppose that a lower level of complexity is provided by the pidgin. This leaves a deficit which the first generation creole speaker has somehow to make up if he's going to acquire a language adequate for expressing all he wishes to express. Well, he may not do anything about the deficit at all. He may just make do with the pidgin. But he doesn't. We've seen this in Hawaii. That is, in Hawaii there's a kind of continuum rather similar, at first sight, to the kind of thing that's been described for Guyana and Jamaica and other similar places. The difference between the Hawaiian continuum and the more familiar Caribbean continua is that really there are two continua, a pidgin continuum and a creole continuum. The pidgin continuum contains a great deal of variation, but it's a kind of sideways variation, if you see what I mean: there's the Japanese speaking one kind of pidgin, the Filipino speaking another, and the Korean speaking yet another. There's not much difference in the depth or complexity of these different kinds of pidgin. The differences in the pidgin continuum are not because one part of the pidgin continuum is further from the superstrate and one is nearer, as is the case in the creole continuum, although you do find that in the creole part of the continuum in Hawaii. The creole part of the Hawaiian continuum is very, very similar to what you find in any of the Caribbean communities. What you find in the pidgin part, you find in *no* Caribbean community for the very simple reason that there the pidgin speakers have been dead for several hundred years. But in Hawaii they're not all dead yet, and that is exactly what enables us to reconstruct the entire cycle. And a full analysis of the entire cycle shows that the axis of variation in the pidgin has nothing to do with the axis of variation in the creole; also there's a structural gap—there are structures which all creole speakers have that no pidgin speaker has. And there are structures that creole speakers have that just a few pidgin speakers have and use very badly, and those few are the pidgin speakers who are the most advanced and out-going within the pidgin-speaking community. Because pidgin speakers vary.

It's a sort of linguistic gospel that all languages are supposed to be equal, all speakers are supposed to be equal. But this isn't true of pidgins. There are certain pidgin speakers who are more outgoing, more open, who pick up more quickly on what's going on. In every case you can look at their life histories and explain why it should be so, because they've had much greater contact with the generations beneath them. What you'll find, if a pidgin speaker has had really intensive contact with his own family, with his own children or grandchildren, or if for some reason something in his life style has involved him very much with younger people, what you'll find is that he will pick up some of the novel creole rules. And you'll find that he'll pick up the surface form of the rule, but he won't pick up the restrictions on the rule. In one case I'm thinking of in particular, a creole speaker might say a sentence like, "Those guys they no like go," with a so-called "pleonastic" pronoun in the sentence. In substandard English a pleonastic pronoun is a topic marker. In Hawaii it's absolutely the reverse. It's a focus marker. And nobody ever described this structure for the simple reason, I imagine, that people thought, "Well, you know, this is just substandard English." Nobody noticed the fact that the function was totally opposite. The insertion of this pronoun depends on one or two factors being satisfied. Either the NP copied must be introduced for the first time in the discourse, or it must be contrastive: "Those guys they don't like, but these guys they do like." So, if either of these two conditions is satisfied, the copying rule applies; if they're not, it doesn't apply. All creole speakers have this rule, and they all apply it beautifully, accurately. The pidgin speaker occasionally has this rule. Most pidgin speakers don't have it. A few pidgin speakers have it—those that do are always putting the pronoun, relativized, in the wrong place. Because when the head noun of a sentence is relativized, you have sentences like, "Those guys play football they no like go," where the higher NP is copied according to the A-over-A principle. But pidgin speakers can't grasp this principle. The pidgin speaker would say, "Those guys they play football no like go," or even, "Those guys they play football they no like go," copying both NP's, that is, if he can use this construction at all, and very few pidgin speakers can even get this far. You just don't find this among creole speakers. A handful of highly, or outwardly, outgoing, extroverted, mixed-up-with-the-younger-generation pidgin speakers have a vague knowledge of the rule, and they might say, "Those guys they play football no like" or "Those guys they play football they no like"—in other words they will insert a copy of the lower noun phrase not knowing it's only the higher noun phrase that has to be copied. So there are quite subtle things, sometimes obvious things, which indicate that the pidgin and the creole are really quite distinct from one another.

Now, what are we to assume? Where did rules like this rule, which copies a certain type of NP and only a certain type of NP, where would something like this come from? Well, it seems to me that there is no more plausible explanation than the following: The child, as I've said, has to make up the deficit, so the child has recourse to things which are somehow already in its knowledge, I mean its innate knowledge of language. It takes whatever the pidgin has, and of course in any given case the pidgin won't be necessarily adequate, and it elaborates it. In the course of so doing it produces relative clause sentences such as, "Those guys play football they no like go." This sentence violates a universal filter proposed by Chomsky and Lasnik, which takes the form *NP [NP tense V].Let's look a little at filters and see what they are and how they're supposed to function.

According to Chomsky, a filter is something a lot like a constraint but not quite so universal in that a filter is something that a child assumes (remember our child selecting, figuring out what kind of language it is that fate has sentenced him to learn by planting him here in Ann Arbor or over there in Paris or in Tokyo, wherever it might be), so he then figures, "Okay [I'm slightly anthropomorphizing Chomsky's account], I will assume that this filter like all the other filters is going to be in my language, unless I get evidence to the contrary," because the filter is something that, again according to the Chomsky and Lasnik paper, a child will assume to be in his language unless he gets evidence to the contrary. Then he will say, "Okay, sentences in this form are out." But if as he grows up he finds himself bumping into sentences of this kind, he'll say, "Oh, hell, I thought it was a constraint, but it's only a filter. So I'll adjust my grammar accordingly, and I'll allow sentences like this since the filter that blocks them can't be in my language." Now then, the question is of course—this is the critical question, and it is a question that I asked Chomsky in correspondence and, oh, I was delighted by the reply, the first time that I ever managed to get a reply like this from Chomsky saying "I really have no answer to this, but it is an important question"—where does the child, the creole child, get the evidence that will teach him not to apply that filter?

Well, he can't get it from his parents or elders, elder siblings, or whatever, which is the way you'd normally get evidence of this kind, because he is the first creole generation. There's nobody higher up than he who can provide him with any evidence. His parents don't produce any relative clauses; how can he get evidence for something like this when his parents don't produce anything like this? He can't get the evidence from all the other languages that are floating around because he's not learning those languages. He's learning the pidgin, he's made a specific choice and he has to learn the pidgin; the pidgin is the only thing that will enable him to communicate with the entire community, therefore he has to learn it, but he's learning from something which would give him *no* evidence that structures of this kind are permissible. And yet he produces them.

Now if this is so, all we can say is that there must be some kind of instruction that tells him to produce sentences like this. What could such an instruction possibly be like? Well at this stage I think we should think our way back down the evolutionary tree for a moment and ask ourselves not just about innate information in human beings but what can be innate in mammalian species or any kind of species, generally. We do know that all species have some genetically wired-in instructions. We know, for instance, that the arctic tern must have some kind of instruction built in that would enable it to fly from the North Pole to the South Pole and back again—that this is not something the baby arctic tern learns at its mother's knee. Its mother doesn't sit there and say, "Junior, you gotta fly north. Be careful, there are cross-winds at such and such a place, and when you see Gibraltar coming up, make sure you steer slightly to the left and keep on going and in a while you'll get there." The migratory patterns of the arctic tern are too important to be left to chance, so they're not left to chance. They're genetically wired in. I'm going to suggest: a) that the instructions about language that we have are too important to be left to chance and are also wired in; and b) that the law of parsimony would suggest that they are instructions of a similar order. Because assuming the arctic tern has some kind of inbuilt instructions that enable it to fly between the poles, one would not suppose that these instructions were in the form of constraints or filters. One would not suppose the arctic tern had an inbuilt constraint which said something like "Don't fly to Australia" and another one called the "Africa constraint" which said "Don't fly to Africa" and a whole series of constraints and filters which would effectively mean the only place it could fly to if it were at the North Pole would be the South Pole and vice versa. One would think that it would have some kind of instruction—of course I'm using the term in a very loose sense—obviously something like sensitivity to the earth's magnetic polarity which has already been shown to be a factor in avian migration, so there would be some particular kind of neural sensitivity to the earth's magnetic field which would in fact condition the arctic tern to fly up and down, rather than across, but this would be—although expressed in terms of the earth's magnetic field and the bird's sensitivity to that field—it would in fact correspond heuristically to a positive injunction to fly to the North or the South Pole.

So it then occurred to me that possibly the kind of blueprint of language that we have wired into our heads is not a blueprint which defines language negatively in terms of formal universals, but rather one that defines language positively in terms of at least certain core structures, certain basic semantic or syntactic structures which are already there. Careful, this is very speculative. It demands that you believe the following: that there is *no* such thing as first language learning. Nobody learns a first language. People already have a first language. What happens is that they grow up and they try to talk their first language and they get hit over the head for trying to talk their first language. They get headed off and steered in the direction of Yoruba, or the direction of Japanese, or the direction of German, as it may be. Just think of this for a moment. I'm thinking of one particularly vivid anecdote, I think by McNeil, which tells the story of a child who says, "Nobody don't like me." And the mother immediately corrects the child and says, "No, little Johnny, it's 'Nobody likes me'." The child repeats "Nobody don't like me." The mother repeats the correction. This goes on for about eight turns. Finally, the child comes up with "Nobody don't *likes* me." The child knows that something is wrong because the mother keeps correcting him, but the child can't for the life of him think what's wrong with a perfectly good sentence like "Nobody don't like me," and therefore he thinks, "Oh, my god, these stupid grown-ups, I'll try and say something that will fit their absurd preconceptions." Now, ask yourself why a child should do this. Why should a child produce multiple negatives which are, of course, also a feature of creole languages, for creole languages form negation in this way too? So why should they do it? Does it involve a copying rule? According to orthodox linguists, it must involve a copying rule because we know that for every sentence there is but one underlying negative. So by this account, what a child must be doing is taking the underlying negative and copying it onto the nondefinite NP. But what other phenomenon in child language acquisition involves learning of a copying rule? The answer of course is none. Is it the case that little Johnny has overheard those wicked construction workers working on the house next door who not only use words with four letters but also say things like "Nobody don't like me"? The answer to that is that in some cases possibly but in other cases almost certainly not, because constructions like this pop up regularly in the speech of children who have been carefully nurtured in lovely suburban homes and who could never possibly have come into contact with anybody who said awful things like "Nobody don't like me." So the child can hardly be imitating. This is one of the things, incidentally, that mothers always explain away by saying this is one of the funny things—not the cute funny things, but the nasty funny things—that the child is always imitating. But is he? In this case I don't think that he is. I don't think he's imitating anybody, and I don't think he's applying some weird ad hoc kind of copying rule either. He is simply producing negatives in the way he was meant to produce negatives—the way God meant him to say negatives. If the sentence contains a negative, then the nondefinite NP must take a negative too. He will only abandon such negative constructions if he is bludgeoned over the head, not only with overt correction, as in this particular case, but also with a whole stack of covert corrections—because he will come across sentences which show that the people in his society don't say it like that. So sooner or later he will adapt what he was trying to say, the way he was trying to say it, into the sentence pattern of this particular community.

So I know of no fact (and I'm hoping in the time for questions later that you will repair my innocence or my ignorance by producing some incontrovertible fact widely known among linguists which is incompatible with this)— as of this moment I know of no fact known to linguistics which is incompatible with the hypothesis that children do not learn a first language, that they have a core grammar that is moderately specified but is obviously not specified down to lexical items, not specified down to phonological rules, not specified down even to low level syntactic rules, but which is highly specified with regard to the core items of syntax, the core items of semantics; and that what happens is, as a child grows up in a normal language-speaking community, he starts to change from these innate rules, to adapt these rules in the direction of the language that he is doomed to learn.

But in a pidgin-speaking community where he can have no correction, overt or covert, he cannot be corrected and therefore does not change these rules. This is one situation in the world that we know of where the children know more of the language than the parents know. How can the parents correct them? They can't correct them overtly because they don't know how to. They haven't the confidence in their own language ability to say, "No you can't say it that way." They can't correct them covertly because they cannot produce the model sentences that the children would need in order to be able to derive rules. So what you have is a child growing up without language correction. And therefore where the child is not blocked by this section, the section of the pidgin that has already been established, where his native responses are not blocked by this, those native responses will come out, and they will contribute to the emergence of a creole language.

The question that now arises is, how would you test such a hypothesis positively? The mere fact that nothing appears to contradict it is obviously not sufficient evidence to show it's true. And it was at this stage that I began to think seriously of expanding the domain of linguistics in the direction of real-world experimentation. And I was fortunate enough to come into contact with somebody else who had also had similar ideas although for different reasons, who was primarily interested in language change rather than the origin of creoles, Karis Talmy Givón of UCLA; and we got together and began to work out how we could possibly test hypotheses of this nature, hypotheses not all of which, incidentally, my co-principal investigator shares. One of the beautiful things about working with real-world experiments is that you don't have to share hypotheses at all. All you have to do is share an interest in whatever hypotheses can be tested and have a willingness to abide by experimental results.

The experiment that we finally decided on was conditioned by a lot of things, and I'll give you briefly just one or two of the considerations that we had to take into account. We early abandoned any idea of trying to actually replicate processes of pidginization and creolization. Such processes, as they have occurred historically, contain far too many variables. In fact that is exactly what is wrong with looking at naturally evolving situations of this kind. We don't know what the really relevant factors were. And the only way to deal with a situation like that is to adopt experimental methods which consist of cutting down variables to a minimum, of getting a situation which is, you know, as much controlled as possible. So let's say if we don't replicate an already existing situation, what do we do? The answer is we try and answer questions about the most significant research issue we can see in all of this. It seems to me quite clear that the research question can only be the following: "Is it possible for members of the human species to produce linguistic rules for which they have no evidence in linguistic outputs available to them, for which they have no evidence in their own language or any language known to them?"

Now we therefore have to put people into a situation in which they are forced to "invent," and thereby see if what they "invent" really turns out to be things that they have borrowed from languages that they already know, or whether their invention contains elements that aren't in those languages, that therefore could only have been drawn from knowledge that, in some sense, they already have. We therefore devised the following experiment: take one uninhabited island in the Pacific. Take sixteen subjects. These sixteen subjects should consist of four subjects each from four different language groups. The four different languages obviously should be mutually incomprehensible and share as little as possible in the way of structure, vocabulary or anything else. They should have, if possible, widely different basic word orders, belong to different families, etc. We decided on four people from each group for a variety of reasons: in the first place, if you have to put people into a situation where they are literally unable to communicate with one another, then that situation is going to be quite traumatic. It would be hopelessly traumatic if in that group there were no one at all that anyone could talk to. So we decided first of all that we would recruit married couples, because one thing we were scared of was producing a Pitcairn Island situation, a situation in which most of the inhabitants succeeded in killing each other off in fights which were mainly over women. Then we learned that in the areas from which we would be recruiting it would be very inappropriate for a male to travel without another male as his companion, or a female without another female as *her* companion; therefore, we would have to recruit two couples from each area, making four persons altogether. Then we were worried about the fact that we would be dealing only with grown-ups, because grown-ups are supposed no longer to have any contact with the *faculté de langage;* at least such contact is supposed to undergo a marked change at the age of puberty. Grown-ups are supposed not to have access to innate language knowledge in the way that children have, and moreover, there's a good deal of evidence that this may be so in the development of pidgins themselves, in the differences between pidgin and creole that I talked about earlier. However, recruiting child subjects is somewhat of a problem in that all subjects are required to give informed consent. You try getting informed consent from a four-year-old. It's not possible. Originally, therefore, we thought we would try the thing with adults because neither of us was really happy with the loss-of-competence hypothesis, loss of access to the *faculté de langage;* and also there was the problem of children getting under your feet, you know, rushing around the island, getting eaten by sharks, and falling out of palm trees—all much more than we could handle. And then I was talking to an anthropologist (because we have discussed this extensively with members of other disciplines, related disciplines in the behavioral sciences), and this man said, "Well, if you recruit childless couples, you're going to get a collection of weirdos." If there is anybody in a subsistence-farming peasant community who is married and who is about that age group (our target age group is 18 to 25) and who doesn't have any children, then he probably has something physically or mentally worng with him and isn't part of an average sample. The natural thing in a society like that is to produce children and plenty of them. So, we thought, there is nothing left for us but to make a virtue out of necessity and say to these subjects, "Well, okay, you can bring your children, provided they're under the age of five, because we couldn't provide them with education, and provided you don't have a horde; if you've got just two or three, that's fine, bring them along."

The proposal then calls for having a community which would consist already of two generations: an adult generation in the 18 to 25 age group, and a child generation in the 1 to 5 bracket. This of course adds another dimension to the whole ballgame because we would have here, side by side, second language acquisition, and first language acquisition, in a test tube under controlled conditions. It involves a lot of additional things such as having someone to look after them and make sure that funny spot is only some little rash and not the onset of some terrifying child disease that would wipe them all out, so we have also budgeted for a nurse who is qualified in pediatrics.

Now, the next thing, when you get these people and their kids on your isolated island, what do you then do? Well, the first thing you do is teach them a basic vocabulary, the reason for this being that you don't want to have them sitting around for the first few months wondering, "Oh what the hell am I gonna call everything?" And you can imagine language chauvinists fighting each other to try and get their own words into the vocabulary. So we thought we'd avoid that by giving them the two hundred or so words that they would most need. These would be, in the main, very simple vocabulary items dealing with concrete objects and so-called "action" verbs. But we would not provide them with any morphology or any syntax. The whole object of the experiment is to see, given this original starter vocabulary, what kind of morphology and what kind of syntax would they possibly come up with? We proposed in the first instance to isolate them for a year, which to many of you may not seem long enough, and it doesn't seem long to me either. The reason for a year is basically that we felt the whole thing was so outrageously novel that if we suggested in the first instance that it would take more than a year, people would just throw up their hands in horror. And, although it may not be adequate, I think a lot will happen in a year. I think certainly enough would happen in a year for us to see if it were going to work out and if in a subsequent experiment it were going to be possible to do this thing for longer.

Anyway, the idea was that at the end of the year there would be a viable contact language, possibly not all that highly developed. But you've got to realize that this situation has certain advantages over the pidgin situation. I think I mentioned this: one of the reasons why I think a pidgin is so rudimentary is that people don't really use it that much or that often. They don't have to. In the average pidgin society, a person can get on well 80 or 90 percent of the time talking to people from the mother country. And pidgin would only be used for that 10 or 20 or whatever percent of the time when it would be necessary to speak to outsiders. Here you have the case where, out of the corps of people, only three will be able to speak your language. If you're speaking to those three persons, okay, but if you're speaking to any of the other twelve people, you have to use the contact language. This would mean that, whereas in the pidgin situation most of the talking is still done in the speaker's native language, here most of the talking will have to be done right from the start in the auxiliary language. I won't go into this in detail, but I have numerous reasons for supposing that the reason why people don't learn languages well when they're grown-ups or don't develop pidgins so quickly when they're grown-ups is because the pressure to change simply isn't on them. Put the pressure on them, and they will develop fast. I hate to use the word laziness, it isn't; it's just natural economy of effort. Nobody puts more effort into any job, unless he is a fool, than the job requires. And so you give him a situation in which he'll make his maximum effort. I think there will be a considerable difference. Even if these people don't make a maximum effort, there are the children, of course, to whom the emerging language will be indistinguishable from any other language. It won't be to them merely some stigmatized form of contact language; it will be the thing that is most useful to them in playing with their playmates, and I think they will also be free of any ethnic feelings that might tend to hold one back from contact with people from other backgrounds than oneself. So you can anticipate probably a more rapid learning, if you can call it learning, more rapid invention going on among the children than among the parents. At the end of the year we will be left, we hope, with a language of some kind. Given this kind of language, what then will we be able to say?

Let me go over some of the more obvious possibilities and show how they relate to significant research questions in the discipline of linguistics.

Now, it's conceivable that at the end of the year we will have a language which simply consists of a kind of patchwork quilt, such as using the rules for the verb phrase from this language, rules for the noun phrase from that one, and some other syntactic rules from a third. You might have some crazy kind of patchwork language which doesn't contain anything that wasn't already in the ancestral languages, the donor languages, the ones that were originally spoken by our subjects. I consider this to be unlikely, but it could happen; I certainly can't rule it out. But if it does happen, it will still not be without interest of a kind. The interest will be exactly: what was it that caused speakers to choose item X from this language and item Y from that language rather than vice versa? Is it the case that this is a purely chance or random process? Is it the case that language is like an erector set, that you can take a bit here and a bit there and put them together and make a new language in any way that you might fancy? It would be an extraordinary finding if you could. I suspect that there are all kinds of hitherto unknown factors that would govern what could go with what—that would prevent any such kind of language from developing. And if indeed our language is made up in this way, there would be ascertainable reasons why certain things were chosen and certain other things were rejected. However, what I would think on the basis of what I've found out in Hawaii, what I think would be more likely, is that there would be at least some rules in the resultant language which could not have been derived from any of the languages previously spoken. And given that there are such rules, then we come to our next big question which is: what, in fact, could those rules be? Would the existence of such rules automatically prove the existence of an innate language capacity? The answer, of course, is that it would not by itself prove any such thing. There would then be two possible positions that could be taken in regard to results of this kind. One could take the position of the empiricists, that if such rules are derived, they are ad hoc conventions, they are things that have been put together to fill gaps in the emerging system, and this has been done by some kind of generalized intellectual faculty that we have. If we assume this, we can make the prediction that in any replication of such an experiment, the original set of rules for which there was no warrant would not recur; that rules would differ in each case depending upon the composition of the group, the language families from which the subjects were drawn, the circumstances in which they were isolated, and a whole range of other possible variables. Every time this experiment was carried out, you'd end up with a different sort of language. However, if one is a rationalist, one predicts the following: one predicts that if indeed under such circumstances speakers produce rules for which there is no evidence in their input, then these same rules would recur and would come up again, over and over again, in any such situation, no matter how different the groups were, no matter how different their languages were, no matter how different the circumstances under which the experiment was carried out were. And if indeed such rules for which there was no obvious evidence were to persist and to reappear constantly in languages of this kind, you would, as I see it, be left with no possible recourse but to assume that those rules were in some sense innate, part of the species-specific endowment with which humans come into the world. So, it can be seen then that experimentation of this nature can bear not only on linguistics, on specifically linguistic problems, but also on the whole nature/nurture controversy, the whole issue between empiricism and rationalism which has remained unresolved for centuries and under present methods of investigation shows absolutely no hope of resolution.

In linguistics as compared to natural sciences, we have been plagued since our birth by an abnormally low level of consensus, by which I mean that there are very few profound or interesting facts about linguistics on which linguists can ever agree. This state of affairs does not pertain in physics or chemistry. But without going into my lecture on epistemology which would take another hour, let me say that I think that this has to do with the fact that one set of disciplines carries out real-world experimentation which actually results in changing the facts that are the subject of debate, whereas ours does not carry out such experimentation. And I think for that reason, once people glimpse the possibility of deciding crucial linguistic issues in this way, that they will not be satisfied simply to allow this to be set aside; and that in the words of Victor Hugo, "There's nothing so strong as an idea whose time has come."

THE GENESIS OF A LANGUAGE
Gillian Sankoff

I'm delighted to be back here at the University of Michigan. I have very good feelings about Ann Arbor, dating from the summer I spent here in 1973 at the Linguistic Institute. What I am going to say today will, I hope, be continuous with some of the ideas that I developed in my Forum lecture here that summer, which had to do with how grammatical machinery is re-modeled in creolization.

I shall begin by sketching my view of the relationship between pidgin-creole studies and the genesis of language. This will be followed by a brief discussion of why the plantation system has been crucial in the genesis of pidgins and creoles. I then turn to Tok Pisin, a language currently undergoing creolization, in order to consider its implications for an understanding of language genesis. Lastly, I review those features Bickerton has proposed as being crucial in plantation creoles, in the light of the evidence of Tok Pisin.

1. Pidgin-Creole Studies and the Genesis of Language

In discussing what we may learn about language genesis from the study of pidginization and creolization, it is important to make clear at the outset that this work has no bearing on the question of the origin of language as it first evolved as a human capacity two or three million years ago. We are talking, rather, about how modern human beings, fully equipped with the modern *faculté de langage,* go about constructing a language.

Most modern humans are, normally speaking, never required to engage in this demanding task, except insofar as we all have to construct our first language (and any other language we learn) from whatever input we receive. Under these circumstances, which we take to be ordinary, we are, of course, required to "construct" something that is virtually identical to a language that, in the institutional sense, already exists. Pidginization and creolization, on the other hand, involve building a language both in the personal and the institutional senses, i.e. building a language that doesn't already exist for a previous generation of speakers. Constructing a language in this special sense, then, involves the genesis of a new set of linguistic practices.

"New" is, certainly, a matter of degree. People cannot build a language out of whole cloth, and are always constrained by the materials at hand. But pidginization and creolization processes *are* qualitatively different from grammatical construction by learners in the circumstances characterized above as "ordinary." Language *change* occurs both in these "ordinary" circumstances and under pidginization-creolization, but only in the latter case do we speak of language *genesis*—this because processes of pidginization and creolization produce such a sharp break in linguistic tradition that their outcome is almost unrecognizable as a product of the preexisting linguistic resources. The materials that are reorganized and remodeled by pidginization and creolization indeed often come from not one but several linguistic traditions, their prior organization and character having been radically transformed.

Before turning to "pidginization" and "creolization" as separate, though related processes, we must consider what kinds of extraordinary circumstances have led people to break so sharply with previous linguistic traditions, replacing them with newly created linguistic practices.

2. Plantations and Pidgin-Creole Genesis

Though the literature abounds with real and imagined cases of language "contacts" (benign and otherwise) leading to language "mixture" of various sorts, the plantation system has for some time exerted a particular thrall in pidgin-creole studies. Reinecke (1937;1938), Alleyne (1971;1979), Bickerton (1977b),Washabaugh (1979), and others have pointed out that the plantation system as it was organized in both Atlantic and Pacific areas has been crucial in the development of "pidgin" and "creole" languages as we know them. I have argued elsewhere(Sankoff 1979a)that in fact we know of no cases where a "pidgin" has developed in conditions other than those of modern European colonial expansion. The plantation system is so crucial because it was unique in creating a catastrophic break in linguistic tradition that is unparalleled. It is difficult to conceive of another situation where people arrived with such a variety of native languages; where they were so cut off from their native language groups; where the size of no one language group was sufficient to insure its survival; where no second language was shared by enough people to serve as a useful vehicle of intercommunication; and where the legitimate language (Bourdieu and Boltanski 1975) was inaccessible to almost everyone.

The languages that evolved as products of these radical, extraordinary circumstances of language contact were to a considerable degree dependent on the specifics of labor organization on plantations. The main distinction to be made here is between the "Atlantic" plantations which used slave labor and the "Pacific" plantations which used indentured labor. The slave labor force was at least to some degree reproduced by "natural" human reproduction, whereas the indentured labor force was almost entirely reproduced by the continued importation of workers on a short-term contractual basis. (Later developments in the Pacific also saw most of the indentured laborers remaining as immigrants.) Contrasting labor policies thus resulted in an early generation of child language learners in the first case, in contrast to their virtual absence (at least during the early period) in the second. The presence of an early generation of children is a key feature in Bickerton's definition of plantation creoles (Bickerton 1977b:57).

Clearly there are many more facts about the way in which plantation labor was organized that bear on our linguistic concerns. One is the relative size of the language groups involved. In Hawaii, for example, heterogeneity seems to have been much less than in the case of Queensland, Samoa, and Fiji in the early period. When surrounded by a sizable group of *wantoks* (Tok Pisin for people who share a language), the pressure on anyone to participate in new language learning would probably have been somewhat reduced, and native languages might survive into first and even second generations of immigrants, with correspondingly greater influence on the evolving creole.

These facts about the plantation labor force (slave versus indentured labor; length of indenture period and presence of female workers; size of language groups) are surely only a few of those that bear on the linguistic products of the plantation system. I think that to understand what happened in any particular case, we must become better historians. We must learn more about the conditions on plantations in order to understand what kinds of communication possibilities existed there, and how these affected pidginization and creolization.

3. Tok Pisin as a Creolizing Language

The object of the research carried out in Papua New Guinea in 1971 by Suzanne Laberge and myself was to study the impact of creolization (i.e. the growth of a community of native speakers) on language change in Tok Pisin. Analysis carried out since that time by us and by other researchers has tended to show that creolization per se has been responsible for fewer of the many developments in Tok Pisin than might have been expected according to the theories of a decade ago. The first part of this section (3.1) will be devoted to a brief presentation of some of the changes that have occurred or are occurring in Tok Pisin. The second part (3.2) will deal with the interpretation of these facts, both in terms of the social history of Tok Pisin and in terms of their theoretical import.

3.1.   Change in Tok Pisin

The seven features of Tok Pisin grammar that will be presented here have all been the subject of full-scale treatment in article or monograph form. Only an outline of each change will be given, along with an attempt to estimate the time frame involved.

3.1.1. Elaboration of Derivational Morphology

Agheyisi (1971:55, as quoted in Mühlhäusler 1976a:240) has stated that for West African Pidgin English the lack of internal structure in the lexicon "single-handedly accounts most significantly for the abnormally reduced size of the pidgin lexicon, the bulk of which is made up of unproductive 'roots' or basic forms." Mühlhäusler shows that this was also the case for "Pacific Jargon English," the predecessor of all the pidgins and creoles of the Southwest Pacific, including Tok Pisin. He states that:

> Its very small inventory of lexical bases and the paucity of lexical information found with these bases [are] a result of the superficial contacts which spawned it . . . . Syntagmatic and paradigmatic relations between lexical items are virtually nonexistent, and lexical items derived by regular processes in the lexifier languages have lost their "transparency."
>
> (Mühlhäusler 1976a:239-40)

Mühlhäusler's dissertation (1976a) is an impressive demonstration of how Tok Pisin has developed its own system of lexical derivation, the three most important types being multifunctionality, compounding, and reduplication (p. 451). For each type, Mühlhäusler analyzes a large number of "lexical programs," which are the actual derivational processes.

Mühlhäusler shows that most of the derivational morphology of Tok Pisin developed:

> At a relatively late stage in its life cycle, when its syntactic structures were already fully stabilized. Thus, any attempt to explain the origin of [its] derivational lexicon in terms of simplifications occurring during the process of breaking down the lexicon of English or powerful influences from various substratum languages during its early stabilization cannot be regarded as adequate.
>
> (Mühlhäusler 1976a:326)

He has, indeed, claimed elsewhere that this is a more general phenomenon, i.e. that "inflectional and derivational morphology are late developments, i.e. they are the first victims of language contact and the last features to be restored" (1979:23). For Tok Pisin, the period in question would seem to be the "expanded pidgin" stage which occurred only after Tok Pisin had stabilized in the early 20th century. Mühlhäusler points out that mechanisms for the formation of lexical items in modern Tok Pisin were not noted by observers writing before 1930 (1976a:326).

3.1.2. The Category of Number

The development of number marking in Tok Pisin has been described in Mühlhäusler 1976b. It appears that *ol* (< Eng. *all*), initially introduced as an optional plural pronoun, later became obligatory as a plural pronoun and was extended for use as a pluralizer with animate nominals. Only later was the use of *ol* again extended to pluralize inanimate and abstract nouns, at the same time becoming "more categorical" with animates. This has led to considerable redundancy as in the following (Mühlhäusler example sentence [35], 1976b:33):

(1) *Sampela ol man ol i save.*
     some–(pl.)–man–they–(pred. mkr.)–know
     Some men know.

As with lexical derivation processes, redundant number marking in Tok Pisin had its origins relatively late in Tok Pisin history. It has developed slowly and in stages. Mühlhäusler concludes that the Tok Pisin number system "is the result of a development which took place when English was withdrawn as a source language. In its nature it is quite different from the English system" (1976b:34-35). (It is important here to note that the withdrawal of English as a source language took place between 1885 and 1917, when New Guinea and Samoa, where many New Guineans worked on plantations, were German colonies.)

Although influence from substrate languages has been shown in the marking of duals and trials, and latterly from English in the optional addition of *-s* by speakers of anglicized Tok Pisin, the way that number marking has evolved to add redundancy in Tok Pisin is specific to its own history and development.

3.1.3. The Cliticization of Subject Pronouns

The particle *i*, now normally analyzed in Tok Pisin grammar as a "predi-cate marker," had its origin in the cliticization of the old subject pronoun *i* (< Eng. *he*), later replaced as a subject pronoun by *em* (< Eng. *him* or *them*). As described in Sankoff 1977a, earliest documents show mainly "bare" subject noun phrases consisting of a noun alone, as in the following:

(2)   *Boatswain gammon me* (Queensland 1885:399, cited in Sankoff
       1977a:63).
       The boatswain lied to me.

The introduction of a redundant subject pronoun seems to have been done for various discursive purposes such as contrast with the subject of a previ-ous sentence as in (3), or disambiguation of long or complicated subject noun phrases:

(3)   Q: *Did you talk to captain at Townsville?*
       R: *No, Jack* **he** *talked* (Queensland 1885:496, cited in Sankoff
       1977a:63).

Later, *i* became almost obligatory with noun subjects and was also intro-duced optionally with pronominal subjects, e.g. *tupela (i) go* 'the two went'. At this stage (the 1920's and 1930's), *i* was reanalyzed as a predicate marker, and the cycle began again, with other pronouns being introduced to accom-pany noun subjects for purposes of contrast or emphasis, as in the following, where the pronoun *em* is inserted between the subject, *meri*, and *i*:

(4)   *Man i-mekim singsing long Mbabmu,* **meri em** *i-go long em, em
       i-pekpek blut* . . .
       Men utter a spell over M.; if a woman goes near them, she will
       have dysentery (from Hall 1943:48).

The *i* particle, having become redundant, is now subject to phonological deletion, so that its presence is no longer obligatory. The whole process has resulted in a complex set of rules having phonological, semantic, and dis-cursive constraints.

3.1.4. The Genesis of the Irrealis Marker [*bai*]

Ross Clark (1979) has shown that an adverbial marker of future time deriving from English *by and by* existed in South Seas Jargon English prior to 1865, and that forms derived from this etymon still exist in the nine Pacific pidgins and creoles he has surveyed (pp. 13-14; 68a). In Tok Pisin, *baimbai* has been reduced to one syllable for most contemporary speakers, and creole speakers often pronounce it simply [bə] (Sankoff and Laberge 1973). In addition, it has moved from sentence-initial position, as in (5), to preverbal position, used redundantly with all verbs marked for future, as in (6):

(5) **Bai** *em kam bek na i stap na kaikai na kisim wara.*
     (Fut.)–she–come–back–and–(pred. mkr.)–stay–and–eat–and
     –fetch–water
     She will come back and stay and eat and fetch water.
                                              (from Mühlhäusler 1979:5)

Note that the verbs *stap, kaikai,* and *kisim* are unmarked. In (6), however, excerpted from a story I recorded as told by an eight-year-old creole speaker of Tok Pisin, all verbs are marked with *bai*:

(6) *Pes pikinini ia* **bai** *yu go long wok,* –**bai** *yu stap ia na* **bai** *yu stap*
     long banis kau bilong mi na **bai** *taim mi dai* **bai** *yu lukautim.*
     You, first son, will go and work in, –you'll remain here and
     you'll stay on my cattle farm and when I die you'll look after
     it.

Bai is also used in the apodosis of conditionals, as in (7):

(7) *Sapos yu no lusim mi,* **bai** *mi kikim yu nau.*
     If you don't let me go, I'll kick you (creole speaker J. P., age 15,
     recorded by S. Laberge).

The transition from adverb to auxiliary would seem to have taken place prior to the 1960's, though a careful historical study has not yet been carried out. Looking for differences between pidgin and creole speakers in the sample of people we recorded in 1971, Laberge and I found no differences pertaining to placement of *bai* or to its redundancy. We were, however, able to show that the creole speakers used more phonologically reduced forms, and tended to unstress it significantly more than pidgin speakers.

3.1.5. The Development of Morphological Causatives

Mühlhäusler has shown that morphological causatives developed in Tok Pisin according to a specific hierarchy, with the suffix *-im* being applied successively to stative-intransitives, then to "true adjectives" (i.e. adjectives that can appear in attributive position), then to nonstatives. He claims that:

> The first morphological causative ending in *-im* is found around 1910, *rausim* 'to throw out' derived from *raus* 'to be outside' (from German *raus*).
>
> (Mühlhäusler 1979:24)

By the mid-1930's, a number of other stative intransitive verbs had undergone morphological causativization, including *slip* 'to sleep, be horizontal' and *orait* 'all right'. Causativized, they become *slipim* 'to make lie down' and *oraitim* 'to mend, repair'. "Shortly afterwards," according to Mühlhäusler, "causativization applies to adjectives such as *kol, sot*, and *bik,* giving *kolim* 'to make cool', *sotim* 'to shorten', and *bikim* 'to make big, enlarge," respectively.

Mühlhäusler explains that the third phase of this development, the application of causativization to nonstative verb bases, really gets underway only in the 1960's, with forms like *sanapim* 'to make stand up, erect', and *pairapim* 'to make belch', and that "the first causative derived from a transitive verb base was found in 1973" (Mühlhäusler 1979:25). He cites the following sentence:

(8)   *Dokta i dringim sikman.*
       The doctor makes the patient drink.

(It should be noted that *dring* is a transitive verb in Tok Pisin, taking objects like *marasin* 'medicine'.)

3.1.6. Complementizer Development

Woolford (this volume) has analyzed the structure of sentential complements in present-day Tok Pisin and has traced the sources of the three complementizers that are in current use: *olsem, na,* and *long.* All three lexical items have other functions in Tok Pisin grammar, but all are subject to reanalysis as verb phrase complementizers under certain conditions (Woolford this volume). For the sake of brevity, and because *na* is less important than the other two, I will discuss only *long* and *olsem* here.

Long, as a general purpose preposition, is often found in contexts like (9):

(9) *Man bilong mi i no save* **long** *tokples bilong mi.*
                    (second-language speaker Elizabeth M., I:1)
     My husband doesn't know (**about, of**) my language.

Woolford shows that the first stage in the transition toward *long* acquiring a complementizer function was the evolution of "a phrase structure rule that expands or rewrites PP as either P NP or P S" (Woolford this volume, p. 111). The following sentence is one in which the sentential complement is preceded by *long,* according to the PP → P S rule:

(10) *Mi amamas* **long** *bekim pas yu bin raitim long mi bipo.*
     I am pleased (**for**) to answer the letter you wrote to me before.
                              (Woolford this volume, p. 111)

Reanalysis of *long* as a complementizer is illustrated in (11), where, as in (9), the verb is *save* 'to know':

(11) *Ol i no save* **long** *ol i mekim singsing.*
     They did not know that they had performed a ritual.
                              (Woolford this volume, p. 112)

Woolford argues that as a complementizer *long* is subject to a deletion rule that does not apply in the PP → P S context. Thus:

(12) *Ol i no save ∅ samting bai kukim ol.*
     They did not know the thing would burn them.
                              (Woolford this volume, p. 112)

The second complementizer, *olsem,* has the broader "meaning" of 'thus, like', and it is used in comparatives as well as in introducing direct quotations. It is a reanalysis of this latter function as that of a complementizer that is of interest to us here:

(13) *Elizabeth i tok* **olsem,** *"Yumi mas kisim ol samting pastaim."*
     Elizabeth spoke thusly, "We must get things first."
                              (Woolford this volume, p. 117)

(14) *Yu no ken ting* **olsem** *mipela i lusim tingting long yu pinis.*
You must not think like/that we have forgotten you.

(Woolford this volume, p. 117)

3.1.7. Relativization

As with complementation, grammatical machinery for relativization is a very late development in Tok Pisin. Sankoff and Brown (1976) also compared data from the 1970's with Hall's texts and other earlier materials, and we found a dramatic increase in the use of *ia* ($<$ Eng. *here*) as a "bracket" for relative clauses. Like Woolford, we also found a sizable increase in the number of relative clauses.

We traced the development of *ia* from place adverb, through demonstrative or deictic, to relative marker as shown in the three following examples:

(15) *Yu stap* **hia.**
Stay here.

(from Mihalic 1957:46)

(16) *Ee! Man* **ia** *toktok wantaim husat?*
(Hey! Man this talking to whom?)
Hey! Who's this guy talking to?

(17) *Na pik* **ia** [*ol i kilim bipo* **ia**] *bai ikamap olsem draipela ston.*
And this pig [they had killed] would turn into a huge stone.

We argued that relativization grew out of the need in discourse for "bracketing" devices for use in the organization of information, and that as the use of Tok Pisin expanded, the slot occurring after *ia* (itself always postposed to the noun it qualifies) was a strategic location for the insertion of further qualifying information. As this information came more and more to take the shape of a full sentence, *ia* became available for reanalysis as a relativizing particle.

3.2. Implications for Language Genesis

Of the seven major developments outlined in 3.1 as having occurred in Tok Pisin grammar over the past century, only the last two—having to do with sentence embedding of various sorts—show a time frame that is possibly coincident with creolization. Each of the other changes seems to have been virtually complete before there existed any community of native speakers. And even for these last two, neither Woolford nor Penelope Brown and I could locate any evidence that native speakers had been the innovators in originating new strategies for embedding.

How, then, are these findings to be interpreted? We had set out to investigate how creolization, i.e. the acquisition of native speakers, was affecting grammatical expansion in Tok Pisin. We found grammatical expansion, but had to acknowledge that most of it occurred prior to creolization. I, for one, had once thought that creolization would be "the crucial case to examine from the point of view of the universals of natural languages—the question being what features are basic to a natural language and therefore would be created at this stage" (Sankoff 1977b:122). But by the time we had finished analyzing the *baimbai* material, I was already unhappy with this view. I thought that it was "vastly oversimplified," suggesting that:

> There may indeed be linguistic features that are characteristic only of languages having a community of native speakers, but this is probably only a special case of the general functional question. A language used in a multiplicity of social and communicative contexts, and which carries much of the "communicative load" for numbers of speakers, will develop grammatical machinery appropriate to its needs. This grammatical machinery will probably be more extensive than that found in a language restricted to a very few communicative contexts that form a small part of any speaker's repertoire of communication situations and that is therefore marginal in terms of usage for all its speakers.
>
> (Sankoff 1977b:122)

Mühlhäusler (1979:3) has made similar proposals. These proposals, however, have to do with only one of the questions the facts about Tok Pisin pose for us, and that is: WHY STRUCTURAL EXPANSION? We have, I think, learned much of what we need to answer this question. Whereas we had thought that the native speaker's "need" to have a fully "natural" human language would be the main force toward structural expansion, we learned that structural expansion is also concomitant with the increasing functional load of a second language.

A useful side benefit of this broadened view has been a better understanding of the relationship between the individual and the community in studies of creolization. In my own and in Mühlhäusler's work, we have consistently talked of creolization as involving a group or community of native speakers, rather than the isolated individual. Though there were isolated individuals

who grew up in families where the parents had only Tok Pisin in common
(e.g. a policeman married to a woman from the area he was posted to), such
persons' "needs" were not sufficient to carry the language, to influence the
mass of second language speakers they were surrounded by. Mühlhäusler cites
an article by Janssen on the plight of racially mixed children in German New
Guinea (prior to World War I), in which Janssen states that "the halfcasts
mostly speak only this Pidgin English with a few bits of native language
heard from their mother, which of course differs according to the home"
(Mühlhäusler 1976a:208, his translation from the German). Mühlhäusler's
comment on this is extremely illuminating, and I quote it in its entirety:

> If Janssen's observations are correct, one is dealing with a situ-
> ation in which children grew up speaking a pidgin as their first
> language without this leading to increased linguistic complexity
> of their speech. If this is true, it would give sustenance to the
> claim that the linguistic expansion accompanying the acquisi-
> tion of a pidgin as a first language is a social and not an individual
> phenomenon, i.e. linguistic expansion only occurs in situations
> where large numbers of first language speakers are involved.
> Creolization is thus the product of "communal language acquisi-
> tion competence." An explanation for this situation may be the
> fact that any improvements a child might introduce as a result of
> his learning a pidgin as his first language are encouraged only by
> members of his peer group who find themselves in the same situ-
> ation whilst being discouraged or ignored by adults.
>
>   (Mühlhäusler 1976a:208)

The difficulties posed by the usual equation of creolization (in the sense
of the acquisition of native speakers) and grammatical expansion have trou-
bled most scholars who have worked on the pidgin and creole languages of
the Southwestern Pacific, and they have proposed several possible ways to
resolve the problem. Clark, for example, has stated that "the simple dichot-
omy of pidgin vs. creole . . . may . . . place unwarranted emphasis on the
importance of the native speaker criterion" (1979:47). Woolford, recognizing
the "differential paths" (Bickerton 1974:24) toward creolization, has suggested that:

> If there does exist some unique kind of language change that
> should be set apart by the label "creolization," it is the case

argued for by Bickerton (1975). According to Bickerton, in situations where children do not have sufficient input from any existing language to learn it as their native language, the children create a new language out of the fragments of the languages they hear plus their knowledge of universal grammar.

(Woolford this volume, p. 108)

She goes on to state that for cases such as Tok Pisin:

The only difference between creolization and other language change (besides, perhaps, the rate of change) is that the normal balance between changes that lead to simplification of the grammar and changes that lead to increased grammatical complexity is upset. The net result is increasing elaboration of the grammar.

(Woolford this volume, p. 108)

Woolford thus expresses the consensus among those who work on Tok Pisin with regard to (a) grammatical expansion and (b) "naturalness" of the changes. The claim for "naturalness" (in a somewhat weaker form, the claim is that changes occurring in Tok Pisin are like "normal language change") is, however, one that deserves further discussion and one that involves the second major puzzle posed by the Tok Pisin facts: WHENCE STRUCTURAL EXPANSION?

Reading the recent literature suggests very strongly that there is also some consensus among researchers about the source of the changes in Tok Pisin. In all the seven publications on which the interpretations in 3.1 are based, the authors manage to propose that somehow Tok Pisin is "going its own way." By this they mean, mainly, that the structures it is developing are not merely calques from either substrate or superstrate languages.

In the case of relatives, for example, Brown and I pointed out (1976:663) that Buang, a New Guinea Austronesian language, has a relativizer that, like Tok Pisin *ia,* also serves as a place adverbial and a postposed demonstrative. Thus:

(18a) *Ke mdo* **ken.**
mi–stap–(long)–**ia**
I live (at) **here.**

(18b) *Ke mdo byaŋ* **ken.**
mi–stap–(long)–haus–**ia**
I live (at) house **this**

(18c) *Ke mdo byaŋ* **ken** *gu le vkev.*

  mi—stap—(long)—haus—**ia**—yu—lukim—(long)—asde

  I live (at) house **that** you saw (on) yesterday.

Hooley (personal communication) pointed out that Buang relatives often also have a closing particle, one of another set of deictic forms, making the construction even more parallel to the left and right *ia*-bracketed relatives in Tok Pisin as in (17) above. Bradshaw (1978) has indeed claimed that the presence of left and right bracketed relatives in a number of New Guinea Austronesian languages makes these a likely source for Tok Pisin calquing. Brown and I felt, however, that there were several reasons why calquing did not provide a complete or satisfactory solution. First, similar structures exist in other, unrelated languages (e.g., Ewe, as described by Benveniste 1957:40), where they have presumably arisen through processes other than calquing on Austronesian. Second, unless relative bracketing is found to be a truly prevalent areal feature, it is difficult to see why any particular Austronesian structure should have dominated, given the very large number of substrate languages involved. As Bickerton, discussing the possibility of African substrate influence, has stated:

> In the highly unlikely event of some African language's being found that showed point-by-point identity with the creole model, "substratomaniacs" would still be faced with the problem of explaining how that language ... could have won out against all competing models, sub- and superstrate, during the period of creole formation.
>
> (Bickerton 1977b:61)

Third, *ia*-bracketed relatives arose slowly, over a period of at least forty years, and the extension from adverb to deictic to relativizer happened in stages. During the first two stages, Tok Pisin contained few relatives, and most were unmarked. Buang speakers I recorded in rural villages in the 1960's did not use *ia*-bracketed relatives in Tok Pisin, despite the existence of relatives bracketed by deictics in their own language and their considerable fluency in Tok Pisin. But urban residents of Lae, including many highlanders with non-Austronesian language backgrounds, used this construction in the early 1970's. The introduction of *ia*-bracketed relatives worked through Tok Pisin by a process of extension from existing constructions, not by a process of immediate calquing of the fully elaborated structure.

Similarly for complementation, Woolford states that:

> The use of *olsem* as a complementizer is quite similar to the
> use of *that* as a complementizer in English, but it is unlikely
> that borrowing was involved. More likely, the similarity arises
> from a similarity of origin.
>
> (Woolford this volume, p. 118)

Woolford cites (this volume, p. 118) a series of sentences from Allen (1977)
suggesting the reanalysis of the demonstrative *that* (OE *ðaet*) as a complementizer (see also Traugott 1972). Interestingly, there are also strong
parallels between the other uses of Tok Pisin *olsem* and Buang *(na)be*, which
is a complementizer as well as an adverb glossing as 'thus, in this manner,
approximately, like'.

Mühlhäusler notes that it is common to find both substrate and superstrate models (or at least partial models) for Tok Pisin structures. In his
analysis of causatives, he shows the existence of structures parallel to those
of Tok Pisin in both English and Tolai. But after suggesting that calquing
from Tolai may have existed at a particular, brief period in Tok Pisin history,
he shows that Tok Pisin took off in its own directions, with the processes
developing in accordance with existing constraints in the language, as well as
following a postulated universal hierarchy as outlined in 3.1.5 above. In his
1979 paper, Mühlhäusler quite clearly lays out the three potential sources
for grammatical elaboration: substrate influence, superstrate influence, and
universal tendencies, in various combinations. I agree with him that these
potential sources will have different weights, and will combine with each
other in different ways, according to the specific historical circumstances and
according to the stage of development of the language.

Certainly the incredible elaboration of Tok Pisin over the past century is
a direct outgrowth of its usefulness to, and use by, many thousands of New
Guineans. As such, it does not provide us with a "pure" case of the unfolding
of universal principles in vitro. People in Papua New Guinea have long had
multilingualism as part of their battery of rhetorical talents, and their knowledge and experience have contributed importantly to Tok Pisin's development. But this does not mean that universal principles have not been at work
in Tok Pisin. My own view is that any language undergoing such rapid and
massive grammatical expansion, and which has had an independent character

as a separate and unitary language from very early on in its history, cannot but proceed to some extent along "universally preprogrammed lines" (Mühlhäusler 1979:35). But note Mühlhäusler's plural: lines, not one unique line. I think that in any area of grammatical elaboration there are several potential natural courses. Perhaps the balance between potential strategies is quite fine, and can be tipped by the presence of some relatively minor factor. If I may be permitted to anthropomorphize a little, I can put it this way. What are the options open to a language looking for a relativizer? There are, I think, only two choices: take a lexical item from the deictic system or from the interrogative system. In other words, if you want to qualify a particular noun, you can either question it or assert it. *Which* N? or *that* N. The balance may have been tipped for Tok Pisin toward "choosing" a deictic by the existence of this pattern in a number of Austronesian languages, but it is also experimenting with a *wh*-strategy, as both Mühlhäusler and Woolford have noted. *We* 'where' is a low-frequency relativizer for some current speakers. The reasons for the greater success of the deictic strategy probably also have to do with factors internal to the language: the fact that the deictic is postposed to the noun it qualifies; the fact that Tok Pisin has no movement rules but generates *we* in the complementizer position (Woolford 1978a, 1978b, this volume). The point is that initial inputs—whether a calque of Tolai causatives or the English order of *here* in constructions like "this X here"—get considerably reworked, in accordance with both natural, universal hierarchies and existing structures in the language.

As a language whose genesis and grammatical expansion occurred largely prior to creolization, but which was nevertheless influenced by universal, natural developmental possibilities, Tok Pisin shows us that adult innovators can be influenced by universals as well as by the patterns preexisting in the native languages they have previously acquired. In the final section, I will look at those features that have been proposed as existing in a set of languages where universals have been thought to have had a freer field (Bickerton 1977b:58-60).

4. Tok Pisin and the Features of Early-Creolized Languages

Strictly speaking, it is both premature and improper to do what I propose to do in this concluding section—premature, because none of the features to be discussed have been the subject of an extensive historical analysis, and improper, because the features in question ought not to be necessarily present in Tok Pisin. They are features Bickerton has found to be strikingly similar in the type of creole Tok Pisin isn't: those early-creolized cases where "the communicational needs of children"(1977b:57)have been the primary factor in actuating the changes. Why I have decided to do it is because in reading Bickerton's list, I was struck by the number of areas in which Tok Pisin showed parallels to the languages Bickerton discusses.

First I should say that there is one feature that is totally dissimilar. Tok Pisin shows absolutely no signs of multiple negation. Tok Pisin lacks the negative indefinites like "nobody" and "nowhere" that in many languages co-occur with negated verbs. Thus 'nobody came' is rendered either:

(19a) *Ol i no kam.*
    They (indef.) didn't come.

or:

(19b) *Wanpela man i no kam.*
    A person didn't come.

or, more usually, it is done by embedding an indefinite (positive) under the negative existential *inogat.* Thus:

(19c) *Inogat wanpela man ikam.*
    There doesn't exist a person who came.

This analysis concords with that presented in Woolford's dissertation, where she argues that "in Tok Pisin there is a maximum of one instance of NEG generated per clause, and that this NEG is generated in the predicate" (Woolford 1977:102). The lexical item *nating* exists, but means 'of no account, to no avail'. Thus *mi wokim nating* means 'I did it unsuccessfully, for nothing', and to gloss 'I did nothing', one must say:

(20) *Mi no wokim wanpela samting.*

The four other areas of grammar all show some correspondence with the patterns Bickerton presents. Focusing, for example, is realized by some form of "left dislocation." This may involve sentences like *meri em i go* 'a woman she goes' (excerpted from [4] above), or it may involve cleft sentences like the following (from Sankoff and Brown 1976:638):

(21a) *Em wanpela America ia [iputim nain long en]* .
    It—an—American—deictic (rel.)—put—name—on—her
    It was an American who gave her her name.

The unfocused equivalent would lack initial *em* and the deictic relativizer *ia*:

(21b) *Wanpela America iputim nain long en.*
     An American gave her her name.

Objects and indirect objects may also be clefted in the same way (with *em* and *ia*), leaving a pronoun optionally for objects and obligatorily for indirect objects. Lastly, objects may be simply preposed, altering the normal SVO word order, as in:

      O   S   V
(22) *Na narapela tu mi stori* (Don D., age 40, recorded by G. S.).
     and—another—too—I'll—tell
     And I'll tell another one too.

In terms of copulative constructions, Bickerton says that "all early-creolized creoles make a distinction between attributive and locative-existential constructions" (1977b:60). He claims that attributive constructions are handled by stative verbs, and that there is usually a distinctive locative copula, separate from the equative copula that occurs in N_N constructions. In Tok Pisin, there is a separate locative copula *stap*:

(23) *Em i stap long haus.*
     He/she is in the house.

But attributive and N_N constructions tend to have identical surface forms. Thus:

(24) *Em i sik.*
     He/she is ill.   (attributive-stative)

and:

(25) *Em i dokta.*
     He/she is a doctor.   N_N

Stap seems to have infiltrated one stative-attributive context, co-occurring with *gut* 'good', but with no other attributes (states):

(26) *Mi stap gut.*
      I am well.

But not:

(27) *Mi stap* $\left\{ \begin{array}{l} *amamas \\ *kranki \\ *sik \\ \text{etc.} \end{array} \right\}$ $\left\{ \begin{array}{l} \text{'happy'} \\ \text{'wrong'} \\ \text{'sick'} \end{array} \right\}$

Another area Bickerton discusses is that of articles. He claims that early-creolized creoles have:

(i) a so-called "definite" article ... which ... corresponds to the semantic category of "existentially presupposed" NP;

(ii) a so-called "indefinite" article ... which corresponds to the semantic category of "existentially asserted" NP;

(iii) a "generic" or "nonspecific" article (zero in all early creolized creoles without exception) which corresponds to the semantic category of "existentially hypothesized" NP.

(Bickerton 1977b:58)

Here again, Tok Pisin's evolution of the past few decades has brought it increasingly into line with the other languages Bickerton describes. Schiffrin's (1976) historical analysis of determiners in Tok Pisin shows that the use of nouns without determiners has declined markedly. Whereas 70.4 percent of the 125 nouns she examined in Hall's (1943) materials had ∅ determiners, this percentage had declined to only 36.8 (of 98 nouns) in my data of 1971. Though ∅ with nonspecific remained constant throughout the period, the use of *ia* and *wanpela* increased in categories (i) and (ii) respectively. *Wanpela* increased from 15 percent in 1943 to 25 percent in 1971, whereas *ia* increased from 11 percent to 43 percent. For *ia* as a "definite" determiner, see examples (6) and (13) above; for *wanpela*, see (19b) and (19c); and for ∅ generic, see (4). Schiffrin's admittedly small sample nevertheless indicates that Tok Pisin is rapidly falling into line with the early-creolized creoles in its marking of nouns. Though the marking of "definites" and "indefinites" is still far from obligatory, the direction of change is clear. Interestingly, *ia* is postposed to the noun, like "-*la* in most Franco-Creoles"(Bickerton 1977b: 58), whereas *wanpela* occurs before the noun like *wan* "in all Anglo-Creoles" (Bickerton 1977b:58).

Finally, we turn to tense and aspect. This is the area for which Bickerton has provided the most detail (1974), and again, we see some close correspondences between the languages he describes and Tok Pisin. Let us examine one by one the characteristics he proposes:

(a) "The zero form of the verb marks 'simple past' for action verbs and 'nonpast' for state verbs" (1977b:58). There are many unmarked or "zero form" verbs in Tok Pisin, and most of them indeed belong to one of these two categories. (One does still find other categories of verbs unmarked, reflecting an earlier stage in the history of the language when there was no verb marking, as evidenced in several of the example sentences in this paper, and discussed in 3.1.4 above.) Unmarked present (ongoing) state is exemplified in (9), and unmarked past action in (11) above.

(b) "A marker of anterior aspect indicates past-before-past . . . for action verbs and simple past for state verbs" (1977b:58-59).

The two candidates for this marker are *bin* and *pinis*. Certainly *bin* is used for past-before-past with action verbs. Verbs with *bin* "denote actions which occurred at a point of time during the nonimmediate past" (Wurm 1971: 47). Here is an illustrative excerpt from a story told by Elena Z., a seventeen-year-old creole speaker of Tok Pisin:

(28) a. *Long taim bifo, ol, wonem,*   Once upon a time, they, uh,
      wanpela ailan,   an island,
   b. *draipela pik i* **save stap** *ia*   a huge pig **used to live** (there)
   c. *na em i* **save kaikai** *ol man*   and it **used to eat** the people
            *****   *****
   d. *Nau, ol* **kisim** *kenu,*   Then, they **took** canoes,
   e. *ol* **stretim** *ol samting*   they **fixed up** all their stuff,
      bilong ol,
   f. *na i* **go painim** *nupela ailan.*   and **went to look for** a new island.
   g. *Na wanpela meri, pik,*   And a woman, the pig, uh,
      pik ia wonem,
   h. **bin** **kaikai** *man bilong en bifo,*   **had eaten** her husband before,
   i. *na em wonem,* **igat bel.**   and she, uh, **was pregnant.**

In this excerpt, the single actions in the past are conveyed by the verbs *kisim, stretim,* and *i go painim,* which are not marked, as predicted in point (a); whereas the past-before-past *bin kaikai* is marked. However, past states are *not* indicated by *bin*—one could not say **i bin gat bel.*

A curious fact about the distribution of *bin* in my data is that its use seems very largely restricted to older men. Adolescent boys, children, and women instead use some combination of *pinis* (whose main function is to mark completive aspect) and *bifo* 'before'. In a sample of eleven speakers I have examined in this regard, the four men all use *bin,* whereas of the seven women and children, only one (Elena Z. in the excerpt cited in [28h]) uses it, once, and then in combination with *bifo.* In the initial "stage-setting" phase of telling a story (for example, referring to an action that had happened before the series of past actions to be recounted in the story), the four male speakers would usually use *bin.* Thus Tony T., a 45-year-old speaker from Buka, explains at the beginning of a story how a *masalai* 'incubus' seduced a man who later died as a consequence of this dalliance:

(29) *Tupela* **bin giris** *wantaim na* **igo wetim** *long rot* **istap,** *long Sarade.*
      The two of them **had flirted** together, so he **went** and **waited** on
      the road, on Saturday.

The flirtation, which had happened before the series of events that began with the man going to wait on the road, is expressed by *bin giris.* In similar contexts, women and children will use *pinis.* John P., a fifteen-year-old creole speaker, takes time at the beginning of his narrative to establish that:

(30) *Nau, tevel meri* **harim pinis.**
      Now the spirit woman **had overheard.**

He continues with his story of how the spirit woman, having overheard some essential information about the plans of two real women, was able to use it to trick one of them.

My feeling about the apparent competition between *bin* and *pinis* is that *bin* is the older form, which may now be losing ground to *pinis.* I do not think it represents a regional dialect, since the four men whose speech I have studied are from four very separate areas: the Highlands, Manam Island, New Britain, and Buka. (A similar diversity exists among the seven women and children who seem to prefer *pinis.*) A full account of the alternation is in preparation. Note that whereas *bin* always occurs preverbally, *pinis* is postverbal.

(c) The irrealis marker is *bai*, as described in 3.1.4 above.

(d) Bickerton discusses a marker of nonpunctual aspect that "indicates both durative and iterative aspects"(1977b:59).In Tok Pisin there are two main candidates for this marker: *save* and *stap. Save* is illustrated in (28) above, marking durativity with *save stap* 'used to live' in line (28b), where *stap* is acting as the main verb, and iterativity with *save kaikai* 'used to eat' in line (28c). Note that the "pastness" of these two verbs is *not* marked, only their durative and iterative aspects. Were it not for the *long taim bifo* 'once upon a time' introduction to the story in line (28a), they could equally well be glossed as present—something like 'is living' and 'keeps eating'.

Despite the attestation of *save* used to mark durativity in (28b), it is in fact largely specialized for marking iterativity, or habitual actions. (Indeed, *save* is probably used exceptionally with *stap* to avoid the infelicitous **stap stap* or **stap istap*.) Continuous or durative actions are usually marked with *stap,* as in the following:

(31) *Ol* **kaikai istap** *nau, disfela meri go insait.*
      While they were eating, this woman went inside.
                              (Paul T., age 11, creole speaker recorded
                                        by S. Laberge 1971:7:2)

Whereas *save* is preverbal, *stap* is usually not only postverbal but clause final, i.e. discontinuous with the verb it marks if that verb is followed by a complement or adverbial expression as in *wetim long rot istap* in (29). *Stap* occasionally occurs preverbally, and Wurm claims that there is a slight difference in meaning between $V + i$ *stap* and *stap* $+ V$. He states that with *stap* $+ V$:

> The focus is on the action denoted by the verb, whereas with $V + i$ *stap,* the focus is on the continuous nature of the action, e.g. *em i stap toktok* = 'he is TALKING', i.e. TALKING is what he is doing; *em i toktok i stap* = 'he is talking', i.e. his action of talking is CONTINUOUS.
>
>   (Wurm 1971:39)

If Wurm is right, it would mean that postverbal *istap* is in fact the principal marker of continuous or durative aspect. In any event, the presence of two separate markers in Tok Pisin means it diverges from the case Bickerton proposes as typical of early-creolized creoles. Interestingly, however, the separation of continuous and iterative categories was a later development in Guyanese Creole as described in Bickerton 1975. The evolution of *save* and *stap* in Tok Pisin is described in Lazar-Meyn 1977.

It should be noted that there are other ways to indicate continuous aspect in Tok Pisin, all of which further emphasize the duration. The three main alternate strategies are: the use of *igo* instead of *istap* as a discontinuous clause-final element; reduplication of the verb; and reduplication of *igo* (I have heard up to six repetitions of *igo*). A wonderful combination of all these markers is found in an expressive passage from a story told by Sarah D., an eight-year-old creole speaker:

(32) a. *Ologeta tupela barata bilong em*   His two brothers

b. *ol* **igo wok finis**   they **had gone to work**

c. *na em wanpela* **istap** *long haus ah,*   and he alone **stayed** home, uh,

d. *insait long rum bilong en* **igo**.   in his room.

e. *Em* **isave pilei** *long das tasol* **igo igo,**   He **would keep playing** in the dust,

f. *em* **isave pilei pilei** *long das, wonem,*   he **kept playing** in the dust,

g. *aninit long haus tasol* **igo** *na,*   under the house, and,

h. *das* **isave kamap** *long skin bilong en*   the dust **would get** on his skin

i. *insait long rum bilong en tu ia,*   inside his room too,

j. *. . . ol das tasol* **isave stap.**   . . . it **was** always dusty.

After the past-before-past in line (32b), Sarah has the following combinations of verbs indicating continuous actions in the past: *istap . . . igo* in (32c) and (32d); *isave pilei . . . igo igo* in (32e); *isave pilei pilei . . . igo* in (32f) and (32g); and *isave kamap* and *isave stap* in lines (32h) and (32j) respectively.

(e) Bickerton says that except for clause external *lo* in Papiamentu, all markers occur in preverbal position. We have seen that this is

not the case for the markers in Tok Pisin, where *bin, bai,* and
save occur preverbally but *stap* alternates, usually occurring post-
verbally, and *pinis* always occurs after the verb.

(f)-(j) Bickerton's remaining points discuss the combinatorial possibilities of the markers which, in all languages he studied, can combine in the order: 1) anterior; 2) irrealis; and 3) nonpunctual. Here
Tok Pisin is quite different. My intuitions are that the following
combinations would be possible, though most are unattested in
my data:

$$\begin{Bmatrix} bai \\ bin \end{Bmatrix} + save + V + \begin{Bmatrix} pinis \\ istap \\ igo \end{Bmatrix}$$

Attested combinations are *bai + V + pinis,* to indicate future perfect; *bin + V*
+ pinis, past perfect; and *save + V + igo,* stressing continuousness. A combination like *bai save karim* 'will be carrying' or *bai lukluk istap* 'will be looking'
would seem grammatical, though in over 400 cases of the use of *bai* I have
examined, I found no such combinations. **Bai bin* or **bin bai,* however,
strikes me as quite impossible. *Bin save V* or *bin V istap* would seem grammatical for continuous actions in the past, though as noted above, speakers
seem to mark only the aspectual quality and leave "pastness" to be conveyed
by the general frame of the discourse with adverbs, etc. *Save V pinis* would
seem another grammatical possibility, but what we get is *save V bifo,* as in
(28) above. As with *bin* and *bai,* combinations of *pinis* with *istap* or *igo*
seem ungrammatical.

I would tentatively suggest that Tok Pisin has some type of constraint
against having two markers in one position, i.e. it doesn't readily allow two
or more markers in preverbal or in postverbal position. This analysis is,
however, very preliminary. The facts are complicated at least by: the use of
save, stap, and *go* as full verbs in addition to their use to qualify other verbs;
verb chaining of types not examined at all here; the existence of other verbs
and markers not discussed here, such as punctualizing *nau,* immediate future
marker *laik,* and "modal" *ken;* and discourse patterns of the "overlay" type
described in Grimes 1972.

5. Conclusion

I conclude that though in many features Tok Pisin seems to have a "core" similar to other creoles described by Bickerton, it has many additional features that give its syntax a unique character, features that are, for the most part, not readily ascribable to either substrate or superstrate influences. Nowhere is this clearer than in the tense-aspect system. To my knowledge, there exist as yet no exhaustive studies for Tok Pisin of the evolution of the features Bickerton has discussed (Schiffrin 1976 and Lazar-Meyn 1977 are initial forays into the history of determiners and nonpunctual markers respectively). It will probably turn out to be the case, however, that like the other features of complex syntax discussed in section 3 above, this second set of features has also evolved slowly in Tok Pisin, and largely prior to creolization. Their source and development must be attributed to an intricate combination of universal and particular influences, and there is clearly much work remaining to be done to integrate the two.

In the evolution of many areas of Tok Pisin grammar, one can observe a series of experiments where people attempt a whole range of solutions to the problem of expressing some meaning or relationship. For the expression of continuous aspect, we noted five such strategies. But one can speak of a grammatical category in the language only when some one strategy has regularized, crystallized, become obligatory and redundant. Though we have seen this happening in many areas of Tok Pisin grammar, the reasons why one strategy has triumphed over another remain to be clarified.

THE GENESIS OF A SECOND LANGUAGE
John H. Schumann

In this paper, I will attempt to address the issue of the genesis of language by examining how four theoretical perspectives in the field of second language acquisition (SLA) account for early sequential bilingualism. Thus, I will discuss the genesis of a second language from Hatch's discourse perspective, Krashen's monitor model, Lamendella and Selinker's neurofunctional perspective, and Schumann and Stauble's acculturation model. In doing so, I will limit myself to the actual genesis of a second language, i.e. the early stages of SLA, and will only tangentially treat subsequent second language development.

THE DISCOURSE PERSPECTIVE

Hatch (1978) hypothesizes that syntax is learned through conversation. The learner's goal is to be able to engage in conversations with target language (TL) speakers. He/she wants to function in TL discourse, and the acquisition of TL syntax is the automatic by-product of learning to do so.

Basing her analysis of second language acquisition data on previous work in first language acquisition (Kennan, 1974; Scollon, 1974), Hatch shows that the learner has three tasks to accomplish in order to "do" conversation. He must get the attention of the person with whom he wishes to talk; he must identify the topic of reference; and he must make topic-relevant responses to keep the conversation going.

The learner accomplishes the first task, getting the listener's attention, in a number of ways. In the following examples Hatch shows learners repeating personal pronouns and proper names and using the exclamation, *oh-oh* (L = child second language learner; TLS = target language speaker):

1. L: (to TLS) *You–you–you–you* (attention getter)
   TLS: *Huh?*
   L: *I–see–you*
       Kenny

2. L: *Ryan, Ryan, Ryan* (attention getter)

3. L: *Oh-oh* (attention getter)
   TLS: *What?*
   L: *This* (points to an ant) (topic nomination)
   TLS: *It's an ant*

(from Hatch, 1978:404)

After getting the attention of their conversation partners, child second language learners often indicate the topic of discourse by pointing to what they want the interlocutor to notice. Other deictics such as *this* or *that* are also used.

4. L: *Lookit*
   TLS: *What?*
   L: *Ball*

5. L: *Oh-oh*
   TLS: *What?*
   L: *That* (points at a box)

6. L: (pointing toward a drum) *This, this, this!*

(from Hatch, 1978:405)

Hatch points out that in first language acquisition there is a progression from verticle structures to horizontal structures. She suggests that the same phenomenon exists in SLA. In vertical structures words are semantically linked in conversational exchanges. The conversation partner, using questions, elicits constituents that fill out the structure. For example:

7. L: *Oh-oh!*
   TLS: *What?*
   L: *This* (points to ant)
   TLS: *It's an ant*
   L: *Ant*

(from Hatch, 1978:407)

Here the L gets the TLS's attention. The TLS asks *What?*; the L points to an ant and says *This*. Then the TLS provides the full target form *It's an ant*. This form then serves as a model for the subsequent development of a horizontal structure which is syntactically linked. Hatch suggests that even though the learner has learned to form syntactic structures in his native language (NL), such structures do not appear in very early second language acquisition because the learner's goal is to learn to do TL conversation, from which TL syntax will naturally emerge. To illustrate, Hatch uses the following example:

8. L: *This boat*
   TLS: *Mm-hmm boat*
   L: *This my boat*

(from Hatch, 1978:407)

Hatch claims that the learner does not simply start with *This my boat* because in "doing" conversation, he must first make sure the person to whom he is speaking has identified the referent of the subsequent discourse. This procedure leads to vertical constructions which will become horizontal constructions when the learner is sufficiently proficient in conversation to incorporate syntactically linked utterances.

It will be recalled that the third task in learning to do conversation is to make topic-relevant responses. Hatch shows that even when the learner knows practically nothing of the TL, he can make conversationally appropriate replies by simply echoing the interlocutor's statements with rising intonation and his questions with falling intonation:

9. TLS: (parking cars and airplanes) *Make it one at a time*
   L: *One at a time?*
   TLS: *Park everything*
   L: /Evrišin/?
   TLS: *Park them*
   L: *Park them?*
   TLS: *Does it fly?*
   L: *Fly*

(from Hatch, 1978:409)

The examples in this discussion have come from conversations with child second language learners. However, the same general argument concerning role conversation can be made about adult second language learners. The only exception is that input to adults often involves the use of more advanced structures and introduction topics which are not identifiable in the immediate environment but which are displaced in time and space. Nevertheless, the use of "foreigner talk" shows how TLSs' sometimes slow rate of speech articulates more clearly and reduces grammatical complexity to make messages clear. It also shows how TLSs make the conversational task (turn-taking) easier for the learner. Adult learners, like children, are attempting to understand and make themselves understood in conversation. Their goal seems to be to communicate; they do not seem to be trying to acquire linguistic rules. However, the linguistic rules which are of interest to gram-marians become evident in the horizontal structures that grow out of conver-sations. So from Hatch's point of view, the genesis of a second language lies in learning to do TL conversation.

THE MONITOR MODEL

Krashen's (1978) monitor model is a model of second language perform-ance which claims that languages are acquired via two systems: learning and acquisition. Learning involves the conscious incorporation of TL rules, and is facilitated by the explicit presentation of those rules coupled with feedback in the form of error correction. Acquisition, on the other hand, is the non-conscious incorporation of TL structures resulting from exposure to and interaction with TL speakers in genuine communicative contexts. The basic claim of the monitor model is that speech is, in general, initiated through the acquired system and that conscious learning is only available as a monitor which can alter the grammar of a TL utterance prior to or after it has been produced.

Monitoring seems to take place only when the learner has sufficient time, and when he is focused on the form of the utterance rather than communica-tion of information or ideas. Current research indicates that for many per-formers, the use of the monitor requires that the focus on form be equivalent to that generated by a discrete point grammar test.

As mentioned above, the monitor model attempts to account for second language performance, not second language acquisition, and therefore it only speaks to the issue of the genesis of a second language in an indirect way. Nevertheless, from Krashen's statements about performance it may be possi-ble to construct a picture of how the monitor model would handle the issue of the genesis of a second language.

Central to the issue of acquisition within the monitor model is Krashen's notion of "intake." Corder (1967) has made the distinction between *input*, which is that language to which the learner is exposed, and *intake*, which is that subset of input that the learner incorporates into his TL communicative system. Krashen (1978) alters this idea considerably and defines intake as "input that enables an acquirer to acquire more of a target language" (p. 15). By this definition intake becomes not those aspects of the TL input which the learner acquires, but rather those aspects of the TL input which facilitate acquisition (a third term needed now to refer to the subset of input that is actually incorporated by the learner).

Thus Krashen maintains that certain forms of input will facilitate acquisition of the TL. He bases this view largely on the research from first language acquisition (Carden, 1972; Clark and Clark, 1977; Snow and Ferguson, 1977; and Newport, Gleitman and Gleitman, 1977), which has attempted to characterize the type of input children receive from their parents, and on research in SLA (Hatch, Shapira and Gough, 1978; Wagner-Gough and Hatch, 1976; and Hatch, 1978) which has attempted to characterize the type of input second language learners (especially children) receive from TL speakers. The input to children acquiring their NL has been referred to as "caretaker speech" or "motherese" and the input to second language is referred to as "foreigner talk." Both these types of input tend to have the following characteristics:

1. They are not used to "teach" language, but rather to get the child to *understand* what is said to him.
2. They refer to the "here and now" and do not refer to events displaced in time and space.
3. They consist of simple-sentences that become more complex as the child develops.
4. They contain syntactic patterns that are frequently recycled.
5. They contain longer pauses which result in slower speech.

On the basis of the findings of input studies, Krashen concludes that optimal input to second language learners, which will constitute "intake," will have the following qualities:

1. It will be *understood* by the learner.
2. It will be just slightly in advance of the learner's current stage of grammatical development. Thus, "if an acquirer is at stage G_i of grammatical development, he or she can progress to the next stage G_{i+1} by *understanding* G_{i+1} syntax with the aid of context" (p. 17). Krashen supports this claim with evidence from first language acquisition (Shipley, Smith and Gleitman, 1969) which indicates that children tune in to input which is at or slightly in advance of their stage of grammatical development

and tune out input that is beyond that stage. Thus in Krashen's view, intake becomes progressively more complex.

3. Intake may be available in natural communcation. Since mothers attempt to communicate with their children and do not try to teach them language, Krashen concludes that intake will be generated in those situations where the second language learner receives comprehensible input in genuine communication with TL speakers.

Using the notions of acquisition versus learning, monitoring, and intake, we can try to generate a picture of how the monitor model would account for the genesis of a second language. A child second language learner coming into contact with the TL might typically undergo a silent period lasting anywhere from one to six months. Krashen hypothesizes that during this period "an acquired competence is built up via active listening until a sufficient 'amount' is present for utterance initiation" (p. 22). Assuming the child has a positive attitude toward TL speakers and is motivated to use the language, he would then begin speaking with some type of simple TL system (or a simple system plus memorized routines). The TL speakers who communicate with him would strike a rough accommodation to this system and would ideally provide input which includes language that is just beyond the child's current stage of grammatical development. This rough accommodation of input to grammatical stage would then continue with each becoming gradually more complex until conformity with the TL standard is achieved.

The situation with an adult second language acquirer might be somewhat different. Communication demands and classroom performance demands which adults face do not generally permit a silent period. The adult then may not have time to develop an acquired competence with which to initiate TL speech. Krashen suggests that under such conditions, the acquirer will use his native language as a substitute utterance initiator and produce TL words with NL syntax. He also suggests that this is especially likely to occur in acquisition-poor environments, i.e. where the learner does not have sufficient access to TL input. In addition, the adult learner, like the child, may resort to memorized routines.

Krashen, citing Hatch, hypothesizes that adults are less likely to receive optimal input. That is, TL speakers do not seem to restrict their speech to either "here and now" situations or to G_{i+1} grammatical sophistication when speaking to adult second language learners.

The adult, on the other hand, may have some access to consciously learned grammatical rules which can be used as a monitor to improve his performance (under certain conditions) and make it appear more native-like. Krashen, however, argues that when the learner is outperforming his acquired competence in this way, he is merely "faking" his performance, and that true acquisition does not take place until the learner's performance is generated entirely through his acquired competence.

In sum then, from the point of view of the monitor model, we see the genesis of language taking place through the interaction of TL input with the learner's acquired and learned competencies. For children, the genesis of a second language occurs through an acquired competence and memorized routines developed during a silent period; when TL speech emerges, it is often supported by optimal input provided by TL speakers. The genesis of an adult's second language may occur through recourse to NL syntax, memorized routines, the application of consciously learned grammatical rules by means of monitoring, and unconscious acquisition from what is often less than adequate input.

THE NEUROFUNCTIONAL PERSPECTIVE

The neurofunctional perspective (Lamendella, 1977; Selinker and Lamendella, 1978) views SLA in terms of the organization of information processing functions in human neural systems. Basic to the approach is Lamendella's (1977) distinction between primary and nonprimary language acquisition. The former refers to the acquisition of one's native language, or in the case of bilingual or multilingual environments, the acquisition of more than one language as a mother tongue. There are two types of nonprimary language acquisition. The first is *foreign language learning* in which the second language is generally acquired through classroom instruction, without regular communicative interaction with native speakers. The second type is referred to as *secondary language acquisition* and usually results from exposure to the TL in the environment in which it is spoken.

Both primary and nonprimary language acquisition take place through the construction and development of neurofunctional systems (NFSs). The approach focuses on cognitive information processing in neural systems and, with regard to secondary language acquisition, maintains that the NFSs which are responsible for this type of language learning are controlled by executive functions which direct second language behavior in three different modes:

1. The first is the *monitor mode* (corresponding to Krashen's notion) which involves the conscious application of learned grammatical rules to the production of TL utterances.

2. The second is the *automation mode* which involves the nonconscious production of TL utterances through automated subroutines (i.e. prefabricated patterns, memorized chunks).
3. The third is the *infrasystem mode* which involves the production of interlanguage utterances through task-specific functional constructs in the brain.

Selinker and Lamendella elaborate in the following way:

> From this perspective, primary language competence of an individual is realized in the Nervous System as infrasystems (more accurately, hierarchies of infrasystems). These acquired information structures are constructed during the process of *primary language* acquisition in conjunction with the progressive *maturational stages* of the responsible NFSs, as regulated by the genetic material. When the need arises to acquire a *nonprimary language* after the period of primary language development, it is almost certainly these same NFSs which (with varying degrees of efficiency and completeness) direct the construction of an alternative set of *nonprimary language infrasystems* (that is, interlanguages [IL]) as the means of producing and comprehending speech in TL communicative interactions. IL infrasystems develop progressively, in *infrastages,* with a more advanced infrasystem taking over prime control of speech behavior from a surpassed infrasystem found to be inadequate (pp. 177-78).

Since the task for this paper is to treat the genesis of a second language, our discussion here will focus on the creation of the learner's initial infrasystems. In very early contact with the TL, before the first interlanguage infrasystem is constructed, the NFSs tend to operate in the monitor mode. This period of the acquisition process is presystematic, and the behavior which results from IL rule schemata (the neurofunctional analog of psychologically real linguistic rules) is not the product of an infrasystem. Selinker and Lamendella describe this as a period of *prenucleation flux.*

Following this presystematic period, the first infrasystem is formed. Selinker and Lamendella see as plausible Corder's (1975) claim that grammatical forms emerging during this period may result from a regression to a stage of linguistic development realized in primary language acquisition. In their terms, such a claim implies "that the executive functions of the linguistic

NFSs apply the same acquisition heuristics which had directed early primary language acquisition, producing IL infrasystems of the same general character as the early infrasystems of primary language" (p. 180). However, for Selinker and Lamendella, learners may vary in the level of the communication hierarchy which is identified as most appropriate for initial IL learning. The learner may opt for a level based on lexicon, operating principles (Slobin, 1973), universal linguistic categories (Corder, 1975; Smith, 1973), or if motivated by the influence of formal cognitive operations (see Rosansky, 1975; Krashen, 1975), he/she may choose the highest levels of language structure as the basis of IL learning.

After continued exposure to the TL, the first infrasystem gives way to a second, more advanced infrasystem. At this point the initial infrasystem remains stored in memory, in latent form. Thus, following the establishment of the initial infrasystems, interlanguage learning may be viewed as proceeding through a series of discrete, autonomous infrasystems with the latest system in the progression generally maintaining prime control over speech behavior, but with earlier infrasystems sometimes reemerging when the learner is fatigued, under pressure, or extremely relaxed. This phenomenon is related to backsliding described in Selinker, 1972.

In sum, the neurofunctional perspective aims at modeling internal (and therefore unobservable) information processing systems. Lamendella (personal communication) sees the approach as equally applicable to primary language acquisition, problem solving, and learning in general. In addition, the approach has been used to hypothesize about the nature of symbolic functions, consciousness, introspection, and the evolution of human language and cognition. The discussion presented above represents the specific application of the neurofunctional approach to second language acquisition. That application results in predictions about interlanguage behavior which now can be examined by the observation of genuine interlanguage productions.

THE ACCULTURATION MODEL

The final perspective from which the genesis of a second language will be examined is the acculturation model (Schumann, 1978; Stauble, in press). This model views SLA as an aspect of acculturation and maintains that a second language learner will acquire the TL only to the degree that he acculturates to the TL group. The model restricts itself to natural SLA that occurs under conditions of immigration to or extended sojourn in the TL country.

When the learner arrives in the TL country and has to or wants to learn the new language, his early linguistic productions will constitute a pidginized system. The typical characteristics of this system as evidenced, for example, in English speech of Spanish-speaking immigrants to the U. S. are:

1. Uniform preverbal negation: *I no can go.*
2. Lack of inversion in questions: *You like this book? Where you are going?*
3. Unmarked form of the verb: *He go yesterday. The boy want a car.*
4. Use of juxtaposition to express the possessive: *the teacher coat.*

This pidginized system appears to be caused by both functional constraints and cognitive constraints. The learner's early TL speech can be viewed as functionally restricted to the communication of denotative referential information. Thus the survival needs of the learner can be met by an essentially unmarked language system. The need for movement transformations that will place the negative particle after the auxiliary in negative sentences and move the auxiliary in front of the subject in interrogatives will only occur when the learner desires to extend his TL speech from strictly referential functions to integrative functions, i.e. when he decides to not only communicate with TL speakers but also to sound like them. It is at this point that the learner will also begin to adopt TL verb and noun phrase morphology.

The cognitive constraints contributing to this pidginized system stem from the learner's inability to deal with the extensive and varied TL input to which he is exposed. The new learner in the TL environment encounters an input overload. He is exposed to an array of grammatical structures and lexicon much too vast to absorb. In order to communicate he is forced to construct from this input a system that will meet his survival needs, and the pidginized interlanguage described above is often the result.

There are several views regarding the process by which this pidginized system is created. The first is that the learner simplifies and reduces the TL input to which he is exposed. He does this by focusing on content words, ignoring both bound and free morphology, rejecting redundancy, and relying on fixed word order. Corder (1975), as mentioned above, argues that the learner does not simplify the TL, but instead produces a simple system through recourse to notions of linguistic simplicity learned in the process of acquiring his first language. The idea is that in the acquisition of one's native language one learns and uses a simple system and from that point on one has access to that system on occasions demanding restricted communication. Thus from Corder's view the learner's pidginized TL speech results from access to an earlier learned simple system lexified with TL vocabulary. Bickerton (see Bickerton and Odo, 1976; and Bickerton, 1977c) views pidginization as SLA under conditions of restricted input. He argues that under these conditions the genesis of a second language involves the gradual relexification of the NL with TL vocabulary. After relexification is completed, native language structures alternate with structures acquired from the TL.

Which one of these processes is eventually shown to be correct is of minimal importance to the acculturation model. What is important is that the model predicts that the genesis of a second language involves the creation of a simple, pidginized system which results from the functional and cognitive constraints which are concomitant with minimal acculturation to the TL group.

In concluding, I would like to explore the questions of whether and to what extent the discourse perspective, the monitor model, and the neurofunctional perspective permit the acculturation model's claim that the genesis of a second language involves the production of an initial pidginized interlanguage.

Hatch sees the very initial stage of SLA as consisting of semantically linked vertical constructions which are embedded in conversations. These forms then yield to syntactically linked horizontal structures. From the examples Hatch gives, it appears that these early horizontal forms often seem to lack morphology, retain fixed word order, and rely on content words in ways characteristic of pidginization:

1. *This +++ noun*
2. *This you?* (= Is this yours?)
3. *Window fish, not window car*
   (= It's a fish tank window, not a car window)

Most of Hatch's examples of the discourse of older second language learners come from a 13-year-old Spanish speaker, Ricardo (see Butterworth and Hatch, 1978). I have argued elsewhere (Schumann, 1978:97-98) that Ricardo's interlanguage was pidginized. He had a *no + verb* negation system; he very rarely inverted in questions; he never supplied the regular past tense inflection and supplied the plural *s* only about 48 percent of the time.

Thus we can conclude that the discourse perspective does allow the view that pidginization can characterize the genesis of a second language, but that the pidginized forms, if they were to appear, would follow vertical constructions which appear even earlier.

The monitor model also permits pidginization to characterize the genesis of a second language. Essential to Krashen's view is the adaptation of the TL speaker's speech to the learner's level of grammatical development. This implies that early SLA constitutes an interlingual system that is simple in relation to the target. The pidginized interlanguage hypothesized by the acculturation model is just such a simple system.

The neurofunctional perspective allows that the learner may choose various levels of the communication hierarchy in early SLA: the lexical level, operating principles, universal linguistic categories, or even the higher levels of linguistic structure. If the learner chooses any of the first three or any combination of them, the likely result will be a pidginized interlanguage.

Thus, all four models permit the view that pidginization may characterize the genesis of a second language. However, only the acculturation model limits itself to this view.

DISCUSSION

How does what I have said this afternoon relate to what Bickerton and Sankoff have said about the genesis of language? Bickerton examines the genesis of language from the perspective of creolization. He sees the child in a pidgin-speaking community having to internalize rules for which there is no evidence in terms of the linguistic outputs of his pidgin-speaking parents (or community). Hence, the child-creolizer resorts to "positive formal linguistic universals" and creates linguistic output to express meanings not available in the input. Bickerton thus sees the child-creolizer as the employer of linguistic universals to create language.

However, in a very recent paper, "Creolization as the Acquisition of a Second Language as a First Language," Roger Anderson (1979) has shown how adult second language learners also arrive at unique linguistic solutions "when they create a non-native form-meaning relationship under conditions of restricted access to the TL norm . . ." (p. 16). In other words, if the genesis of a second language produces the pidginized IL that the acculturation model predicts, and the learner only has restricted access to target language input, the need may arise for him to call on his "positive formal linguistic universals" to create linguistic forms to express form-meaning relationships which are not available in the restricted TL input to which he is exposed. Thus the adult second language learner/pidginizer (like the child-creolizer) contributes to genesis of language not simply by producing a pidginized interlanguage but by creating linguistic forms. Anderson offers the following examples:

A. The use of **for**:
   1. *He is* **for** *school* (= teacher).

2. *You* **for** *me* (= and).
3. *He* **for** *long hair ties it.* (= He ties back the long hair.)

B. The use of **stay**:
   4. *Never in my life I* **stay** (= have been) *in an accident.*
   5. *I* **stay** (= have been) *here 35 minutes today.*

C. **Is** and **was** as preverbal markers of tense:
   6. *That room* **is** *belong to Christine, too.* (= That room belongs . . .)
   7. *That part on top* **is** *go down.* (= That part on top goes down.)
   8. *The house* **was** *belong to his son.* (= The house belonged . . .)
   9. *I* **was** *live in New York about six years ago.* (= I lived . . .)
   10. *I* **was** *be a student all my life.* (= I have been . . .)

D. Incipient Modal Auxiliaries
   1. *The question that I* **supposed** *to ask you is* . . . (= A question I suppose I can ask you is . . .)
   2. *He* **suppose** *in this time drinking a cup of coffee because he like coffee.* (= I suppose he is drinking coffee . . . OR He must be drinking coffee . . . OR He is probably drinking coffee . . .)

All these created forms are used sporadically and inconsistently in second language learner speech. But we can imagine that they might be used much more generally and consistently if the second language learners had to use the TL for communication among themselves and not just with TL speakers. Then if the learners' children were to acquire this speech as a first language, they might adopt the forms, regularize them, and where necessary go on to create new ones.

Thus in the genesis of a second language, a simple pidginized system may be produced. If the learner is cut off from TL input at this stage, he may have to create forms to express certain meanings. In a sense he has to become an adult-creolizer who employs the "innate positive formal linguistic universals" to which Bickerton refers. But whereas Bickerton restricts this process to child-creolizers, there is evidence that it also occurs in the genesis of a second language by adults.

Gillian Sankoff has pointed out that in Tok Pisin, which existed as a pidgin for a long time before it creolized, the innovations (i.e. the creative work) took place in the pidgin. During creolization the children then do a lot of phonological reduction on the innovations created in the pidgin. Thus we are left with the following sources of innovation in the genesis of language:

1. As shown by Roger Anderson, innovations can be generated in SLA, but they are used sporadically and inconsistently.
2. As shown by Gillian Sankoff, when the SLA context is also a genuine pidginogenic social context (i.e. tertiary hybridization) and when pidgin exists for a long time before creolization takes place, then the innovations will be consistent and regular in the pidgin and will be phonologically refined in the creole.
3. As Derek Bickerton has shown, when the SLA context is a genuine pidginogenic context and the pidgin creolizes early, some innovations will be introduced in the pidgin, but these will be added to, extended, and regularized in the creole.

Thus it would appear that access to linguistic universals is possible in SLA, pidginization, and creolization, but in each situation the degree of access varies.

THE SYSTEMS PERSPECTIVE: THE GENESIS OF LANGUAGE
Rodney Moag

0. **Introduction.** This paper has a two-fold purpose: Section 1 will deal with certain important points relevant to the theory of pidginization and creolization which have emerged from my work in the South Pacific and elsewhere. Pidgins and creoles, despite their uniqueness with regard to internal structure, are subject to the same laws and processes as all languages in social context. Pidgin and creole linguistics will be advanced by giving recognition to the common ground shared by pidgin and creole theory and the sociology of language.

Sections 2 and 3 have a rather different purpose. In them a model of language acquisition and performance is presented based on the analog of electronic communications systems. The main function of this exercise is to demonstrate the theoretical possibility of a single language acquisition/ performance device which would operate to produce most of the observed, or posited, phenomena relating to the genesis of language—the theme of the present series. A list of topics relating to this theme appears in Table 1. Obviously a series of five papers could not hope to deal with all, or even half, of them. Other contributions deal with topics 4 through 8, covering the areas of pidginization, creolization, and language acquisition, particularly of a second language. I shall also include Topic 9, the formation of nonnative varieties of English, or of any second language. These three topic areas, then, are those which will be highlighted in the discussion of the explanatory power of the proposed model in Section 3.

1. **On pidgins and creoles.** The careful and extensive research of Derek Bickerton and Gillian Sankoff on creole and postcreole situations and on New Guinea Pidgin in transition from a pidgin to a creole respectively has resulted in invaluable contributions to the field of pidgin and creole linguistics and, particularly in Bickerton's case, to more general linguistic theory as well (see especially Bickerton 1973). The conclusions of highly specific research often tend to be generalized, however, in ways which are not supported by the narrow data base employed.

Bickerton (1977b:49), for example, defines creolization as "first language learning with restricted input," pointing out that it involves the formation of "rules of language that are not derived from any linguistic input"(1977b:64). It is his position that children who are acquiring a pidgin language natively

TABLE 1

Related Topics

1. Development of communications systems by hominids.
2. Divergence of genetically related languages over time and space.
3. Results of language in contact.
4. Formation of pidgins.
5. Extension of communicative function of language: pidgins, vernaculars, and standard language.
6. Creolization of a pidgin, or other L2.
7. Second language acquisition.
8. First language acquisition.
9. Formation of nonnative varieties of English, or of any second language.
10. Formation of special argots, jargons, etc.
11. Creation of artificial languages (Esperanto, etc.).
12. Idioglossia (language devised by identical twins).
13. Creativity in expression and usage by practitioners of oral or written literature (poets, raconteurs) in L1 or L2.

Some Operating Principles of the Systems Perspective

1. Duplex system with independent decoding and encoding.
2. Necessity for operating power: optimal, minimal, and excess.
3. All input and output signals as energy which is either conducted or dissipated or stored.
4. Cumulative nature of deposits into the memory.
5. Importance of monitoring the performance of the system through hard-line feedback.
6. Capability of controlling one infra-device with another or by self-adjusting circuits.
7. The system's capability to generate its own signals under certain operating conditions.

generate rules to express meanings which are not present in the restricted pidgin of their model-providing parents and that these rules often have their genesis in linguistic universals inherent in the innate language competence of the species (1977b:65). All of Bickerton's examples involve three areas of syntax from Caribbean, Indian Ocean, and Hawaiian creoles which "show grammatical similarities not far short of identity in several areas" (1977b:58).

Information in Sankoff's paper in this series furnishes direct counter-evidence to Bickerton's defining characteristic of "limited input." She reports that parents speaking New Guinea Pidgin (NGP) as an L2 exhibit no less syntactic elaboration than their creole-speaking children. Thus, in the very area where Bickerton sees creativity as a necessary part of the creolization process, namely, syntax, there appears to have been none in the creolization of NGP. What is more striking is that Sankoff indicates that most of Bickerton's categories within his three syntactic areas—articles, tense/aspect, and focus (1977b:57ff.)—which he posits as reflecting cognitive universal categories applied by the creolizing child as a result of restricted linguistic input, also exist in the nonnative speech of NGP-speaking adults. One counter-example, clearly, does not totally invalidate Bickerton's very attractive theory, but it does mean at the very least that restricted input and the result-ant generation of rules not derivable from the input cannot be a defining characteristic of creolization.

Creolists have, in general, sought to establish the uniqueness of pidgins and creoles as language types dubbing them "unnatural languages." This has caused them to overlook the ways in which these languages, set off by more recent and distinctive birth and by sparseness of syntax, follow the same laws and processes as "natural languages." Alleyne has taken a major step in his paper by recognizing that the linguistic situations of various creoles in different parts of the Caribbean have grown out of the differences in the language contact situation in each area. (See Moag, forthcoming c, for a more general discussion of the correlation of language situations with socioeconomic conditions.)

One factor deserves special mention here, i.e. what Ferguson (1977:44) has called the "state of development" of a language to its use and function within the society. The degree of use within each domain and subdomain of activity and the total number of domains in which the language operates will determine its range of expression, or what Robson (1975) calls "effa-bility." Wurm (1977:334) characterizes NGP as having approximately the same range of expression as a vernacular. Bickerton (1977b:57), himself, recognizes NGP as perhaps possessing "optimal levels of effability" but does not seem to realize that this would mean unrestricted input for the child learning NGP as his L1.

Once a pidgin has become creolized, it may be structurally distinct but sociolinguistically indistinguishable from other languages occupying the same functional slots in society. Creoles soon develop an oral literature and become associated with other elements of culture such as creole dance, special religious practices (Voorhoeve 1971:310), food, etc. Mihalic speaks of language loyalty for NGP even among second language speakers (1971:xv). Where a creole exists in relationship to an apparently related standard language—what DeCamp (1971b) calls a postcreole situation—the creole functions precisely as do genetically related dialects to their standards. I have pointed out (Moag 1977 and forthcoming a) the feelings of diglossic Hindi speakers in both India and Fiji that their dialect (low variety) is a corrupted and debased form of the standard language. Precisely the same feelings are reported for creoles when they are in a postcreole situation or diglossic situation with English or French. Moag and Moag (1977:21) report similar feelings of illegitimacy toward an informal nonnative variety of English which developed on school playgrounds in Fiji.

In situations where the creole does not operate in a relationship to an apparently related standard, it functions as a vernacular rather than a dialect (see Stewart 1968:537 for the distinction between dialect and vernacular). In Surinam, Saramaccan and Javanese occupy the same functional territory for their respective groups. Thus, the term creole can have reference only to certain characteristics of internal structure and to the historical antecedent of a language, but not to its sociolinguistic status or function.

To further document the "natural" behavior of creoles, they can, like any other language, be extended into new and more formal domains of activity such as creative writing, the church, governmental activities, the media, etc. Voorhoeve (1971) presents an interesting scenario of the progress of Sranan first into the church, and then into other domains of formal activity. Wurm (1977) and Moag (forthcoming b) provide information on the relative penetration of pidgin into formal domains in New Guinea, the Solomon Islands, and the New Hebrides, and the varying degrees of expansion required in each case. Far more is involved than simply adding to the lexicon through coinages and borrowings. Stylistic variants are differentiated, new discourse and rhetorical norms are created, syntax is often somewhat elaborated, and so forth.

The progress of a language from pidgin to creole status is mentioned by nearly every writer in the field, but attempts to define this growth in quantitative terms are very scarce indeed. I found the lexicons of fluent outgroup speakers of Pidgin Hindi (PH) and Pidgin Fijian (PF) in Fiji to consist of little more than one hundred items. In addition, the PH speakers had a single grammatical morpheme (the verb marker *oo*) while PF speakers had both a noun marker (*na*) and an all-purpose tense/aspect marker (*sa*). Nevertheless, with this limited lexicon, speakers were able to discuss everyday topics and even recount incidents from their personal experience. One can imagine even much smaller lexicons being functional if the language were used solely in the marketplace.

The next identified stage on the route to creole status is that of expanded pidgin (Todd 1974:70) which Bickerton, for some inexplicable reason, finds meaningless(1977b:56). Samarin(1971:119) reports that his tally of over 700 basic morphemes in Sango, a widely used Central African pidgin, was roughly equal to the number which Swadesh found for natural languages. Therefore, in the transition from a basic to an extended pidgin, there is at least a seven-fold jump in the number of basic morphemes, to say nothing of all the other trappings of language which must be acquired in the bargain. Taylor (1978) showed how early Hiri Motu had far fewer function words than the thirteen set forth by Dutton (1978) for its present expanded descendant. Sankoff and LaBerge (1973) traced the historical development of the segment *bai* from a sentence adverbial in final position to a tense/aspect marker moved to within the verb phrase. More such studies will help to clarify the nature of the elaboration which accompanies the expansion of a pidgin.

Nonnative Englishes, like pidgins, have their genesis in the contact situation. Wherever the British, or Americans, set up colonial rule, a rather limited, formal variety of English was learned by a small number of locals. Though less restricted in form than a pidgin, this variety was for these users quite restricted in function and usually limited to work-related contacts with the native-speaker colonial masters. When speakers of various local languages brought into close contact by the new situation began using English to communicate with each other in non-work-related domains for which the previous English experience had provided no input, a similar kind of creative activity took place in expanding these new varieties of English to full effability as has been mentioned for pidgins above. (This scenario is outlined much more fully for nonnative Englishes in Moag, forthcoming b. Something similar must have taken place for Spanish in areas of Latin America with large indigenous populations.) Since users of nonnative English, like users of pidgins, have to find representations for semantic relationships and generate rules not present in their linguistic input in the process of elaborating their second language, this capacity must also be accounted for in an adequate model of the language performance.

The one difference which Sankoff notes between L2-speaking parents and L1-speaking children of NGP is in the area of low-level phonology, i.e. of reducing disyllabic function words to monosyllables, and of reducing monosyllables in terms of stress level and vowel quality. More data are needed to assess the real significance of these changes, but two possibilities present themselves. They might reflect permanent change in the phonological shapes of these few morphemes across one generation. Alternatively, and I suggest more likely, these are the kinds of phonological reductions which typify casual speech varieties. (See Moag 1973 for a treatment of phonological processes in casual speech.) Casual speech styles are especially prominent among teenaged speakers such as those Sankoff had as her NGP creole informants. It is further possible that we may have an additional instance of the operation of very general sociolinguistic principles in the transition from extended pidgin to creole. I have pointed out (Moag, forthcoming d) that one of the defining differences between a native and a second language variety of English is the relative lack of casual or rapid speech forms in the latter. We need to see whether Sankoff's teenaged L1 NGP speakers would use the same reduced forms of the function words in writing or in making a welcoming speech to a visiting dignitary. The fact that *baimbai* is always used on the radio, whereas *bai* is found in conversation (Sankoff and Laberge 1973:77) indicates that stylistic variation already exists in NGP at the lexical level. The existence of marked styles would be one further piece of evidence that NGP is no longer a true pidgin. Samarin (1971:122) says a pidgin speaker "is limited to the use of a code with but one level or style or key or register." Pidgins can have phonological variants, however, conditioned by the L1 phonology of various groups of users. I have reported the differing phonological characteristics of Indian versus Fijian users of PF (Moag 1978:78ff.). Fijians, Indians, and Chinese also have distinctively characteristic phonological renditions of PH. These are not stylistic variants, however, as an individual speaker controls only one and cannot switch varieties according to context.

Natural languages have more than one style (Hymes 1967:9), and this is another way in which pidgins may assume the characteristics of natural languages during the course of their elaboration. I have demonstrated (Moag, forthcoming b) how the extension of nonnative English into informal domains of activity in Fiji and other former colonies has resulted in the formation of a clearly distinct stylistic variant of the indigenized English used there. Platt (1978) has called such a basilectal variety in Singapore a "creoloid."

An interesting example of stylistic divergence is the development of Church Creole when Sranan began to be used in the churches of Surinam and then subsequently spread to other formal domains (Voorhoeve 1971:309). More sociolinguistically sensitive observation of other pidgins and creoles will help to confirm whether stylistic differentiation is a concomitant of the functional extension of language in general.

Having shown that pidgins and creoles share some of the same sociolinguistic processes with "natural" languages, I would like before closing this section to deal briefly with a few misconceptions commonly encountered in the literature regarding the genesis of pidgins in particular. Hall (1962:152) and DeCamp (1971a:22) among others declare that a multilingual setting is essential for the birth of a true pidgin. Fiji is a clear counterexample. Though PF may date back to pre-European times (Geraghty 1978), it came into general use as a contact code between Fijians and Indians after Indians moved onto leased agricultural plots near Fijian villages following the fulfillment of their terms of indenture on the sugar plantations (Moag 1978:87). Though some of the Indians had other mother tongues, they all knew and used Fiji Hindi, the L1 of some 75 percent of the community, which functioned as the lingua franca of the community. Similarly, though Fijians have very distinctive regional dialects, many knew colloquial Bauan (or Standard Fijian) which was the code of interregional contact for the larger Fijian community, as well as being the mother tongue of some 15 percent of Fijians. Therefore, in terms of intercommunal contact, there were only two languages. Out of this essentially bilingual setting came not one pidgin, but two. This two-way pidginization stems from the fact that neither group was superordinate. Whinnom's (1965) tertiary hybridization did not operate since they did not take the language of the colonial rulers, English. The fact that PF was based on a standard language and that PH was based on a dialect shows that the lingua franca function of the source languages was dominant over the factor of prestigiousness since Standard Hindi was also available as a potential source. The fact that pidginized varieties were employed by L1 speakers attests to the desire of both groups to maintain social distance (Hall 1962:153).

Lastly, this offers proof on two counts that the basic forms, at least, of this pidgin were provided by ingroup members (Fijians), and not through the inept mimicry of outgroup members (Hall 1966). The phonology and lexical items found in PF are those taken from Standard Fijian, markedly distinct from the words and sounds which Indians would have heard listening in on the conversations of their Fijian neighbors in the regional dialect. Secondly, PF uses special emphatic forms of the personal pronouns, again in Standard

Fijian phonology, which they would not have heard in the everyday conversation of Fijians, even in the colloquial standard. Naro (1978) has documented that the Portuguese themselves simplified their language in order to teach it to West Africans brought to Lisbon in the 15th century which gave rise to Pidgin Portuguese. Bickerton gives this fact little importance stating "there is good reason to suppose that pidgins would turn out the way they do irrespective of whether their speakers were offered simplified or nonsimplified models"(1977b:50).The type of input presented to the learner of a pidgin may not affect the form which that language takes in his output, but as shall be seen in Section 3.2 below, it does mean that very different processes would be set in motion within the language acquisition/performance device which has significance for the purposes addressed in the remainder of this paper.

2. **The operating principles of the model.** The model of language acquisition/performance described below was worked out through the application of the systems design approach. In said approach the designer says, "We want a device which will accomplish tasks A, B, and C. What components will the device need to have, and in what configuration must the components be arranged in order for the device to perform all the tasks well?"

The seven operating principles discussed below are well-known characteristics of electronic communications systems, or parts thereof. Brief examples of each as they apply to electronic devices are provided, as they can, in most cases, help to illuminate the more abstract way in which the same principles operate within the proposed model. The linguistic analogs of each principle are spelled out and, where necessary, the way in which the principles are incorporated into the model. References to the components of the system will, in the main, apply to the simplified diagram of the system appearing in Figure 1.

2.1. **The duplex nature of the system.** Most two-way radios and home intercoms are simplex in nature. Press the button to talk; release it to listen. Only one of the activities can go on at a time. In contrast, the telephone is a duplex system with which you can transmit and receive (talk and listen) simultaneously. Here the parallel with human language performance is plain enough. We can still listen, albeit less attentively, during our own speech production. One of the main functions of the control center (see Figure 1) is to distribute the energy supplied by the power source proportionately to the transmit and receive sides of the system, depending on which activity, or mode, is dominant at the time. During speech, full power is fed to the transmit side of the system with reduced power going to the receive side. On the

FIGURE 1

LANGUAGE ACQUISITION/PERFORMANCE
(Simplified Model)

AUDITION

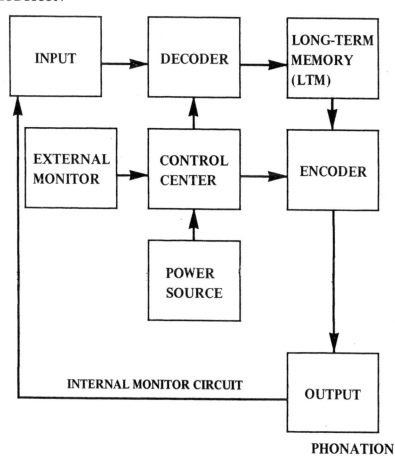

PHONATION

other hand, when listening is dominant, full power goes to that side of the system, though a fair amount of energy may still be required by the transmit side for formulation, and often the conscious review, of upcoming utterances. Occasionally incoming information may be processed and stored during actual speaking time, but completely bimodal activity makes very high demands on the power source and expends the available power at an accelerated rate. Simultaneous interpreters, for example, have a very rapid fatigue rate. Occasionally TV newscasters have tried to free themselves from the written script or the teleprompter by prerecording their commentary and listening to it through a flesh-colored earplug and simply parroting what comes into their ears a few syllables or words later. Try it sometime, and it will become obvious why the method is not widely used; it is very enervating. The capacity of the system for duplex, though not fully bimodal, operation requires that the functions of decoding and encoding be handled separately by discrete devices within the system.

2.2. **The need for operating power.** Whereas certain individual electronic components such as diodes, resonant circuits, and antennas can operate solely from the energy of a signal supplied to them, all major components of a communications system require operating power to do their work. The transistor radio or walkie-talkie cannot operate without batteries, or some other source of electrical power. Such devices have an optimal operating power, at which they are designed to operate best; a minimum operating power below which they cannot function normally; and a maximum operating power which, if exceeded, causes either damage or erratic behavior of the device. A radio designed to operate on six volts (four 1.5-volt batteries) will operate optimally at that power level. If we connect only three batteries, supplying only 4.5 volts, the operation of the set becomes minimal. Even with turning the volume full on, only the strongest stations will be heard. As the power drains from the batteries and the voltage falls even lower, the few stations which can still be heard are no longer clear but become distorted since the minimum operating power level has been surpassed.

Operating power is just as essential to the language performance system as to the piece of electronic apparatus. The precise biological nature of the energy source which powers our linguistic competence is a detail which need not concern us here. What is important for the present discussion is the principle that the processes involved in language performance require power in order to operate. Furthermore, the power is gradually consumed by the operation of the system, just as the batteries for the transistor radio eventually run down. Energy is thus temporarily exhaustible, but in the human instance, at least, is also, happily, renewable.

We have no ready means for measuring the level of human energy as we can with a battery, but the operation of the language performance system is clearly related to the amount of energy available. The optimal energy level is that at which the language user has full access to all aspects of his linguistic competence—essentially faultless functioning of all language-related skills, control of all styles of the language, etc. When less than optimal energy becomes available, either through the power requirements of other non-language-related tasks or through the natural process of fatigue, linguistic performance deteriorates. The first things to suffer are the more complex skills of learned second langauge competence and control of the most formal styles of the L1. Soon the ability to decode heavily content-laden linguistic input (the kind which cannot be handled by preprogrammed infrasystems) and the ability to encode and transmit discourse-relevant utterances go down as the level of fatigue increases. Below a certain energy level we find it next to impossible to carrry on even the most elemental linguistic activity.

Slowly increasing the power to our transistor radio beyond six volts (by adding extra batteries, etc.), we would find that the set operates normally, perhaps apparently better than normally, with a slight boost in power. Beyond this level, however, various squeaks and squeals and other unwanted signals will appear across the dial. The set might even "take off" into self-oscillation, motorboating, or other unwanted activities. The maximum power level may also be exceeded for the language performance system, though perhaps not with quite such dramatically aberrant results. Such phenomena have been studied little, but most of us are personally familiar with the sometimes unpredictable linguistic outputs which result from trying too hard or from being extremely emotionally wrought-up, both of which probably make excess levels of energy temporarily available to the system.

The application of slightly more than normal energy can result in what are generally regarded as creative uses of language—the clever turn of phrase or pun, the extension of meaning of a word or structure, etc. Excessive energy levels, however, seem to engender misinterpretations of strings, the production of unrelated discourse, poorly encoded or articulated utterances, and the like.

The integral nature of a power source in human language competence seems not to have been recognized. For this reason the correlation of energy level to the performance level of language competence has been little discussed in the literature. Plainly this is an area which needs much further investigation. It will be shown in Section 3.2 that certain activities may be highly energy-consumptive though they might not appear to be, namely, the pidginization stage of second language acquisition (SLA) where the system must deal with an unmanageable level of input.

2.3. **Input and output signals consist of energy.** Not only is energy required to operate the system, but what passes through it in the way of signals is energy as well. Acoustic signals striking the eardrums are converted into neural (electro-chemical) energy and apparently remain in this form. Encoded utterances reach the speech organs in the form of neural energy which is then converted into acoustic signals by the movements of the speech mechanism. As signals pass through the various parts of the system, they are subject to the same laws which govern the behavior of signals in electronic communications systems, i.e. they may either be conducted, dissipated, or stored.

In terms of linguistic behavior, conduction is easily envisioned. Energy passes through the input circuits to the decoder where it is split in various ways with the separated discourse functions, semantic relationships, lexemes, grammatical and phonological processes, being stored in their respective areas in the long-term memory (LTM). During speech production, a signal is built up through the retrieval of various components of the types just mentioned, combined in the encoder, and dispatched through the output circuit to the speech mechanism. Some discussion of how energy may be dissipated within the system apppears in Section 3.2 below. The storage of energy is treated next.

2.4. **The cumulative nature of stored deposits.** As utterances are decoded, each component as isolated by the decoder is stored, as outlined in the preceding section. Many items in each category—discourse, semantics, lexicon, syntax, and phonology—will be deposited over and over again as they occur and reoccur in the input to the system. (Input consists both of audited utterances of others and of monitored utterances through the feedback line, or internal monitor circuit, described below.)

The common storage device for electronic energy is the capacitor. Before long the charge begins to "bleed off" gradually, eventually diminishing to a very low level. New applications of energy are required periodically, like the redeposits into our long-term memory, in order to keep the capacitor fully charged. Thus it can be seen how those items and processes in frequent use would be redeposited often enough in the LTM to maintain a full level of energy in their stored state. Such entries would present strong signals to the various retrieval devices associated with the encoder and would be easily picked up, even at relatively low levels of operating power. Scans for common items, or for common strings stored whole by infrasystems (see Section 3.3 below), would require relatively little energy from the power source (as administered through the control center), whereas peak power would be required to retrieve the relatively weak signals presented by infrequently deposited items and processes. Once a little-used item or process is redeposited, its stored energy level remains higher for some time, but unless reheard or reused, will return to a very low level as before. One might alternatively posit a memory which works analogously to magnetic recording which is used in audio archives and in computer storage banks. In such a system, each deposit would have to be made in a separate storage space and the features of cumulative deposits and gradual bleed-off of deposits would not apply, and the model would lose some of its explanatory power. The energy is probably at least partially depleted when an entry is retrieved for use in an utterance, but it will be restored to its previous level by being redeposited again through the monitor line to be described next.

2.5. **The importance of monitoring.** Most systems have specific means for monitoring the most critical aspects of their operation. Electronic, and other, equipment is fitted with meters, warning lights, oscilloscopes, and the like. Within the proposed system of language performance, some of the internal functions of the system are optionally available through the conscious review devices associated with the control center (shown in Figure 2). Continual monitoring of the output of the system is accomplished through the internal monitor circuit (in both Figures 1 and 2). One tends to think of the monitoring of speech as acoustic in nature, the sounds from the mouth traveling along the cheeks and entering the receive side through the ears, or perhaps more directly through cranial bone conduction. Though this kind of monitoring is secondarily available under normal conditions, it serves only to provide feedback on phonetic accuracy of articulation, appropriateness of supersegmentals, suitability of speaking volume, and the like. Such features might seem really to be a part of the functions of the external monitor described in detail in Section 3.1. The primary monitoring of the discourse relevance and well-formedness of utterances is of necessity carried out by an internal connection. You can speak, for example, in the presence of an overpowering noise such as that generated by heavy machinery or a loud rock band which would totally mask your speech, even to your own ears. Still you would be aware of what you were saying through the internal monitor circuit which carries the utterance, in the form of neural energy, from the output back to the input.

2.6. **The capacity of the system to adjust itself through internal means.**

FIGURE 2
LANGUAGE ACQUISITION/PERFORMANCE (Detailed Model)

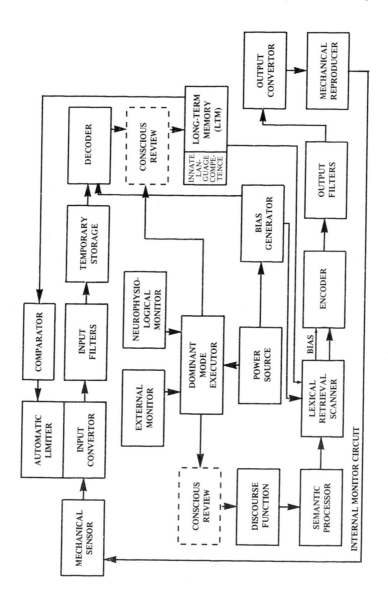

Electronic equipment today is replete with self-adjusting, self-limiting circuits to make its operation more stable as well as easier for the consumer. TV sets adjust their color automatically; FM receivers have automatic frequency control which keeps you perfectly centered on the station as you tune from one edge to the other; tape recorders have circuits which automatically adjust the record level according to the loudness of what is being recorded.

The language performance system can adjust itself in many ways to accommodate special conditions. As L1 acquisition progresses, we obviously adjust the input and output filters to pass only a certain range of phonetic shapes. A new accent or speech defect we are not used to gives us trouble until the system readjusts itself to incorporate these new variations within the range accepted by the input filter. Children who have difficulty with specific sounds can, apparently, program their lexical retrieval scanner not to bring up words containing these sounds. We will see below how the system adjusts itself in the face of overwhelming L2 input. Finally, when we have determined what is discoursally or otherwise significant to our purposes, it is possible to adjust the decoder to respond only to these, or especially to these, depending on our particular needs. So important is the limiting of various devices within the system that a special device called the bias generator has been included for the purpose (see Figure 2). This device can apply energy to the decoder, the encoder, and various retrieval scanners so that their operation will be limited. Police monitor receivers and many two-way radios have a knob labeled "squelch." When the squelch is in operation, the receiver is silent until a signal comes on the channel. If the squelch knob is set nearly to "off," the weakest signal will open the receiver and be heard; but if the squelch is fully on, only very strong signals will open the receiver, and all others will be unheard. It can be seen that scanners could similarly only pick up entries with the highest stored energy levels (most commonly used items) if a heavy control current were placed on it by the bias generator which could happen, among other times, in cases of severe emotional stress.

2.7. **The ability of the system to generate forms not in the linguistic input.** The ability of the idealized native speaker to produce strings in his output which had never occurred in his input was much referred to by the proponents of generative grammar and is almost universally acknowledged. Useful and notable though this "generative capacity" may be, it has little significance for the genesis of language since it really consists of making new combinations and permutations of items occurring in the linguistic input according to rules, conventions, and constraints which govern as well as inhere in the prior linguistic input. Just how these constraints are deduced from the raw data is beyond the state of our art at the moment, but that it happens is no longer questioned.

What concerns us here is the ability of a language user to innovate beyond the limits of previously acquired rules. I have already referred in Section 1 to some of the ways in which both first and second language speakers apply creative energies in order to broaden the expressive range of a language which is moving into new functional territory. This has taken place with highly restricted pidgins, with creoles, and with standard languages where a limited formal variety has been learned in school. It happens in L1's where children learn a very restricted pidgin from their parents or in the cases of dialects, vernaculars, or standard languages where writers, public speakers, and others develop new usages and set new norms within the language.

There are several ways in which electronic communications systems can generate outputs and otherwise exhibit performance not intended by their designers, each having linguistic parallels. It is possible for the language performance system to be overloaded at its input either by loud noise which is disorienting, or by linguistic input which is very different in character from the usual ones, and thus nearly impossible for the system to handle. It is also possible, as mentioned in Section 2.2 above, for the system to produce unwanted signals through the application of excessive operating power. Finally, and perhaps most significantly, is the tendency of many circuits, particularly amplifiers, to go into some form of self-oscillation when provided with full operating power, but with no input. Similar conditions would occur in the language performance model when, in the course of encoding an utterance, there are no stored ways of realizing a particular discourse function, or semantic relationship, or no lexical items with appropriate semantic readings. How the system might generate its own signals is discussed in Section 3.4 below.

Finally, it is often the case that signals passing through electronic devices acquire harmonics or other less systematic by-products including a certain amount of distortion, all of which were not present in the signal at the input. The nature of such changes and their intensity with relation to the basic signal will be largely a function of the characteristics of the individual components of the system through which they pass. Such phenomena could, on the one hand, account for some of the idiolectal variation found in language; their more important implication for the genesis of language seems to be in the area of language change, particularly in the areas of phonology and word meanings.

3. **The explanatory power of the model.** It will not be possible in the

present paper to address each of the points (Table 2) which the model purports to account for. Instead, four topics will be treated which, when taken together, facilitate an exposition of the overall system and its most notable components. The reader should familiarize himself with the eight components of the simplified diagram in Figure 1 before proceeding to the much more detailed diagram in Figure 2. The long-term memory and the control center may be clearly seen as the heart of the system in Figure 1. In Figure 2, innate linguistic competence is set off as a subdivision of the long-term memory, whereas the control center is divided into the dominant mode executor, the bias generator (see 2.6 above), and the two conscious review devices in the receive and transmit lines respectively. Both the input and output circuits from Figure 1 are broken down into components in Figure 2 to reflect the conversion from acoustic to electro-chemical energy at one end and vice versa at the other, and to indicate the filtering at both input and output which are required to make the system language-specific.

The process of encoding is seen to take place in a given order, reflected by the sequence of the various retrieval devices in Figure 2. In order to eliminate unnecessary complexity in the diagram, these same separate functions of discourse, semantics, lexicon, grammar, and phonology were not shown for the decoder or for the long-term memory. Other components will be discussed adequately in the following subsections.

3.1. **The preeminence of communicative goals.** The discourse perspective of Hatch (1978) holds that the basic goal in L2 acquisition is to be able to converse with L2 speakers, and that the acquisition of L2 syntax is a by-product of pursuing these communicative goals. In the model two separate monitors feed information to the dominant mode executor (DME) on the basis of which the DME schedules activities in order to meet communicative goals. Whether one's goal in SLA is integrative or instrumental (Lambert 1972) or expressive (Pride 1978), the system must be operative and, more often than not, in communication. The neurophysiological monitor transmits the physical and emotional needs of the speaker to the DME—hunger, desire to get someone's attention, the wish to assert oneself, feelings of anger or joy, and so on. The external monitor furnishes information on the situation in the external environment such as what the desired addressee is doing, what other activities are in progress at the time, when is the appropriate moment to take the floor, etc. Under normal conditions, such information from the external monitor allows the DME to determine when to pursue the goals, communicative or otherwise, which the neurophysiological monitor expresses. In extreme cases, however, the signal from the neurophysiological

TABLE 2

EXPLANATORY POWER OF THE MODEL

The following reported phenomena can be accounted for:
1. Preeminence of communicative goals (Hatch 1978).
2. Why children do not adopt motherese or foreign accent of parents.
3. Plateauing in first and second language acquisition.
4. Pidginization stage in L2 acquisition (Schumann 1978).
5. Progressively more complex stages in L1 and L2 acquisition.
6. Lag period during which additional items and rules can be decoded but not available in the output (Krashen).
7. Backsliding to earlier, simpler stage of acquisition (Selinker and Lamendella).
8. Below-competence performance by L2 learners:
    a. In the classroom;
    b. On exams;
    c. On the street and on their feet.
9. Lessening of formal stylistic features and reversion to informal style by native speakers under duress: pain, fatigue, grief, etc.
10. Disparity between input and intake (Corder).
11. Employment of special simple register by L1 speakers under marginal communications conditions.
12. The ability to create representations not found in the input for meanings already in the Long-Term Memory (Todd 1974; Wurm 1977).
13. Availability of grammar as monitor (Krashen).
14. Higher overall competence in L1 in areas such as:
    a. Quicker rate of decoding and encoding;
    b. Greater recovery of intelligence under marginal conditions, i.e. interference;
    c. Immediate recall of longer sequences in L1 than in L2.

monitor is so strong that it overrides the input from the external monitor, and the speaker cries out in pain, yells in anger or defiance, or calls for milk while someone else is talking.

In more general terms the external monitor is the device which permits the individual to internalize the code. Code is used here not as used by many sociolinguists to mean the language itself (Gumperz 1968:464) but as used by Halliday (1975) and others meaning a system which is above language including such things as logic, social hierarchies, natural world orders, the nature of things, etc.

The external monitor does not consist solely, or even principally, of the sense of hearing, but is a complex device processing information from all the five senses, passing the compiled data on to the DME. Measuring the data from the neurophysiological monitor against those from the external monitor, the DME orders the discourse function device to select an appropriate function based on the discourse constraints stored in the LTM. From this point on, the assemblage and encoding of utterances proceeds in the manner indicated by the sequence of retrieval devices in the transmit side of the system in Figure 2. The topic of the discourse might be supplied system-internally, i.e. by the speaker, or might be supplied by another interlocutor and conveyed to the system through the external monitor.

Once the discourse topic has been encoded within an utterance designed to accomplish the already determined discourse function, the utterance can proceed straight through the output circuits, where it receives final phonetic shape, to be articulated by the speech mechanism. The order to begin utterance, as mentioned earlier, is issued by the DME based on information supplied by the external monitor. In some instances prospective utterances will be subjected to conscious review for overall appropriateness to the intended discourse function, conformity to constraints in the code, semantic accuracy, grammatical well-formedness, etc. The conscious review devices from the receive and transmit sides both connect into the DME so that a postulated utterance may be measured against previous incoming utterances for conformity to broader discourse constraints. If found adequate, a reviewed utterance may be then sent on and launched. If found wanting, it could be recycled for modification. If found to violate major constraints, it could be discarded and the assemblage/encoding process initiated afresh. Of course the conscious review devices require extra energy from the power source when operating, thereby draining the source more rapidly. One of the reasons why L2 performance is much more fatiguing than L1 performance, particularly when the speaker has learned rather than acquired L2 competence (Krashen 1978), is the tremendous need for conscious review not only in appropriateness to discourse function, but more especially for grammatical and phonological well-formedness.

There is a difference in accessibility between learned and acquired competence which may not be fully accounted for in this system. Grammar rules in learned competence, which, incidentally, exist for L1 as well as L2, may be specifically articulated in the process of reviewing utterances before launching or may be used to edit existing utterances in a written or oral text. The rules in acquired competence, on the other hand, may be employed but not consciously articulated. Further, there is a complex area of sociolinguistically conditioned behavior which appears to be a part of acquired rather than learned competence. Children with one or more parents with a foreign accent or speech defect under most circumstances will begin to follow the norms of other speakers around them in preference to those of the linguistically unique parent. Mature speakers with full acquired competence make selections of rhetorical norms, lexical items, grammatical structures, and phonetic shapes to produce styles of language appropriate to a wide range of social contexts. Since the contexts are external to the speaker and always in a state of flux, the signals for activating the array of special rules required to produce a given style must be given at an early stage in the utterance generation process almost certainly by the DME, and unquestionably on the basis of information supplied by the external monitor. Like other acquired competences, even when utterances are subjected to conscious review and approval for stylistic appropriateness, the rules to which the potential utterance conforms are beyond review. Underlying all of the production of utterances, however, whether reviewed or not, is the preeminence of discourse norms which often coincide with Hatch's communicative goals.

3.2. **Pidginization of L1's and L2's.** Schumann (1978) holds that the pidginization (essentially lexical only) stage is the essential first stage of L2 acquisition for immigrants or sojourners to a target language (TL) country. According to his theory, input overload forces the learner to devise the pidginized system in order to meet his basic survival needs. His contribution to this series also shows how three other perspectives on SLA allow for, but do not require, the pidginization stage—the discourse perspective (Hatch 1978); the monitor model (Krashen 1978); and the neurofunctional perspective (Selinker and Lamendella 1978). This section first explores how the model accounts for pidginization in L2 acquisition, then shows further how the system can also account for intentional pidginization by L1 speakers.

3.2.1. **Pidginization in SLA.** At the beginning of the L1 acquisition the filters are wide open, letting anything and everything through. Gradually, as the phonemic, phonetic, and other rules of the L1 are acquired, the filters become programmed to pass signals on the basis of their possession of the phonemically distinctive features. Even after the filters are fully programmed, constant monitoring of the input is carried on by the comparator which examines the incoming signals and scans the long-term memory for similar segments, strings, intonation patterns, etc. If a particular input signal is identified as L1, or as familiar nonlinguistic information—a dog's bark, the horn of a car, or what have you—the signal is allowed to pass through the filters to the decoder for further processing and deposit in the LTM.

If the input is identified as unfamiliar, however, it is marked as unprocess-ible, and the automatic limiter (duplexed to the input convertor in Figure 2) goes into operation to limit the signals which the convertor allows to pass into the rest of the system. Limited by power from the bias generator, the input convertor tries to isolate an identifiable segment or sequence which it then passes on to the filter at low level. The stranger the shape of the isolated segment, the more its energy level, already weak, will be attenuated in passing through the filter. Next the decoder, which has been biased to greater or lesser degree, tries to assign a semantic reading to this very weak, oddly shaped segment. This will require heavy reliance on the external monitor for contextual cues. The segment will be deposited in the LTM at a very low energy level, making its subsequent retrieval very difficult when needed for an utterance. Under such conditions a segment will need to be forced through the system numerous times before it achieves full energy status in its stored state. The acquisition of each segment (lexeme) will require both time and energy, and a lexicon of fifty to one hundred words would be very costly to acquire. Gradually, however, such a lexicon can become a functional part of a subsystem within the learner's linguistic competence and, with a minimum of syntax, can be used to meet his basic needs. (Neurolinguistic evidence indicates the existence of separate systems for true bilingual speakers [Paradis, personal communication]. It seems logical that there would be a common input circuit, however, which would identify the incoming signals as Lan-guage A, Language B, or unknown, then route them to the filter in one or the other system. With all other L2 users, however, it seems that a single system is in use.)

Alleyne (this volume) feels that Schumann's acculturation model has no relevance to pidgin and creole theory since the learners are immigrants to native TL-speaking lands. I disagree. Chinese have been resident in Malay-speaking territory at least since the 15th century. Many have learned only the pidginized Pasar Malay, whereas a smaller group, the Baba Chinese, has developed a distinctive creolized version. Indians have lived in Fiji since 1879 and only have learned PF which is now being replaced by English in the present generation owing to mass education. Part of Schumann's theory is that social and cultural distance from the dominant group is the principal reason why many immigrants do not pass beyond the pidginization stage of SLA. This is nothing but "keeping the other group at arm's length," one of Hall's (1962:152) functions of a pidgin.

3.2.2. **Pidginization of L1's.** A pidginized variety may result, as shown in the preceding subsection, from the attempts of outgroup members to deal with an overwhelming body of TL input. On the other hand, as discussed in Section 1, such a variety may result from the desire of L1 speakers to engage in no more than basic communication with outgroup members, thereby maintaining social distance. In such a case the task is made easier for the learner as his linguistic input already appears in the form of isolated segments provided by the L1 pidginizer. Consider how the native speaker might generate this highly restricted output. Whereas in Hatch's discourse model the goal of the learner is to keep the conversation going, in the minimal contact situation the goal of both L1 and L2 speakers is to accomplish some sort of transaction, either social or economic. Conversation becomes mainly instrumental in function. Despite the apparent differences in the two situations, what Hatch calls the task of denoting the topic of reference (1978:405) is common to both. It would be the denotation of the topic of discourse, I suggest, which has lead Fijians, whose language is VOS, to adopt SVO order when pidginizing. In fact, subject initial order is the one concrete suggestion of a universal operating in pidginization set forth in the "lexification theory" in Moag (1978). In addition to topic comment ordering, it may also be universal in pidginization to begin the comment with the verb. Speakers of Hindi, an SOV language, put the verb in medial position not only in PF but in PH as well.

In a true pidgin, there are really very few questions of syntax to be resolved. In Krashen's monitor model learners are characterized as applying native language (NL) syntax to TL lexemes. This is clearly an overgeneralization. Some of the examples in Schumann's data appear traceable to NL syntax, but others do not. The pidginizing L1 speaker would treat the pidgin as another, more distinct, stylistic variant of his L1, the special rules for which would be set in operation by the DME by information supplied by the external monitor. The encoder would be heavily biased to block all higher syntactic processes.

There is much debate as to why certain forms and not others become included in a pidgin. As with most phenomena related to language, a single explanation cannot account for all cases. In terms of the pidginizing L1 speaker, his goal of carrying out a social or economic transaction with a nonspeaker would motivate him to seek for ultimate economy of lexicon. The DME could order a scan of all the whole utterances stored in the discourse sector of the LTM (see Section 3.3 below). This would yield a list of items not based on absolute frequency of occurrence, but on maximal combinability with other elements and in various syntactic structures (I am indebted to T. L. Markey for this suggestion). This would explain the choice of objective over nominative pronouns in so many European-based pidgins, though they would probably also win out in terms of absolute frequency or emphatic nature. The selection of the low frequency emphatic set of pronouns over the much more common nonemphatic set in PF shows at least one case where emphasis won out over frequency.

In the case of the outgroup member trying to learn enough of the pidginized L2 to carry out his transaction goals, two possibilities are most likely. The most highly stressed items would get through the heavily biased input circuit more easily than others and would be deposited in the LTM at higher energy levels. The most frequently occurring items would build up high energy levels in their stored state more quickly, thus becoming available for retrieval for speech production, and hence sooner for the resultant maintenance of their high stored level. Pidginizer and pidgin learner would both tend to reinforce those items used most frequently by the other, including common syntactic patterns. The processes are thereby set in force for institutionalizing a specialized language variety highly restricted in form.

3.3. **The acquisition of language in progressively complex stages.** I have already referred to some aspects of the longitudinal operation of the system. Full power is required for the very limited operation of the system in the initial or pidginization stage of language acquisition for reasons spelled out in Section 3.2.1 above. Gradually less power is required to process the very limited amount of input which has actually become intake at this stage (see Corder 1967 for the distinction between input and intake). As the filters become partially programmed, the decoder becomes able to assign semantic readings to the lexemes routinely, and these same lexemes plus the basic ordering rules reach reasonable energy levels in the LTM, thus becoming retrievable for speech production.

A second stage begins when the comparator is able to recognize stage 1 data easily and can, therefore, reduce the bias to the input circuits permitting slightly more of the input to become intake. Along with tagging old items, the decoder is now able to research (through the external monitor) new items and to begin to look at syntactic processes. Until the new stage 2 elements have achieved a certain energy level in the LTM, the learner will have only passive control of them. This accounts for the "silent period" as outlined by Krashen (1978). Around the time when active control is achieved over stage 2 intake, the comparator begins to recognize the items and strings in question, and further reduces the bias to the input thus opening the way for the beginning of stage 3 intake and its processing.

No attempt has been made here to define these stages precisely in terms of the observed sequence of acquired competence in language acquisition reported in the literature. With the model proposed, it appears at this writing as though this would be a straightforward exercise at least for L1- and L2-learning children. The picture is often complicated for L2-learning adults for whom learned competence plays a major, often dominant, role. Even in these cases it seems likely that the acquired competence for these learners, minor though it often is, would follow the same line of progress through stages of increasing complexity for child learners. The details of the intake (particular lexemes, discourse functions, syntactic processes, and the like) would doubtless differ between children and adults.

3.4. **Backsliding and regression.** It has already been shown that newly acquired items have a lower energy level in their stored state than items acquired at earlier stages. It has also been seen that the system would be able to retrieve only the strongest items from the LTM under conditions of fatigue or when the available power to the system is curtailed for other reasons. The same end result occurs when bias is applied to the scanners (see Section 2.6 above) under emotional stress. These reflect two ways in which the system could produce utterances conforming to the rules of an earlier stage of acquisition rather than with those of the present one, i.e. backsliding or regression (Selinker 1972).

The third source of backsliding relates to the neurofunctional perspective of Selinker and Lamendella (1978), one of the features of which is the creation of "infrasystems" which handle specific linguistic tasks on a semiautomated basis. They theorize that these are developed at various stages of language acquisition, then superseded at successive stages by new infrasystems which more perfectly conform to the rules of the target language and contain fewer features of the interlanguage.

Infrasystems are accounted for by the model at two levels, semiautomated and fully automated. So far in the description of the operations of the system, the emphasis has been on the handling of single utterances by disecting them and depositing the component parts into respective sectors of the LTM. This is necessary in order to develop a generative competence. For discourse purposes, whole utterances and interchanges between two external speakers are frequently monitored and stored in toto. An important part of acquiring the "code" in the Hallidayan sense consists in learning what kinds of initiators are appropriate to various stimuli, etc. Such stored sequences would not necessarily be faithful reproductions of the form in which they were originally uttered, of course, being subject to distortion and misreading in the input and to cumulative deposit of interlanguage utterances produced by the speaker, or by other speakers in the case of nonnative Englishes. The discourse function scanner could, therefore, supply previously heard or used utterances whole to the DME which could be transmitted as is. This constitutes a semiautomated system still requiring participation of the DME, but requiring less energy to operate than systematic assemblage which requires the participation of all components on the transmit side of the system.

Fully automated infrasystems operate through the comparator. In scanning the LTM for familiar strings, the comparator must go to the discourse sector, since in no other portion of the memory are whole utterances to be found. Along with the stimulus strings which the comparator is searching for will be stored one or more appropriate responses which can be sent straight to the output circuit with no order needed from the DME. This process would require very low energy consumption since so few components of the system are actually involved. Conscious review before launching would not occur with either type of infrasystem.

There is no evidence that the system has the capacity to erase stored data, but only to reinforce it through repeated deposits, amend it through additionally acquired readings and rules, or to let it gradually bleed off to a low level of stored energy. Consequently, infrasystems from earlier stages of acquisition will not only be present in the LTM, but often at high energy levels. The most systematic backsliding would be that where a much-used utterance from the preceding stage of active competence is stronger, hence more easily retrieved, than a less-used one from the present stage. Infrasystem utterances from even earlier stages could survive for a very long time since their reuse at later stages would keep their stored energy level maximal. The strongest items tend to be retrieved when power to the system is reduced, and the conditions under which backsliding generally occurs—being fatigued, emotionally disturbed, or extremely relaxed—are precisely those which make reduced power available.

3.5. **The capacity of the system to generate signals not derivable from**

the input. In Section 2.7 above three conditions were mentioned under which the system can produce outputs not derivable from prior inputs—excess operating power, input overload, and no excitation. The latter is perhaps the most interesting for it holds the possibility of allowing innate language competence to come into play. For example, in the assemblage process the lexical retriever might encounter no lexeme with the desired semantic reading. On the other hand, given appropriate lexemes, there might be no formula for encoding a particular set of semantic relationships. Under these conditions, with full operating power applied to the system but with a particular retrieval device drawing a blank, categories could surface from the more deep-seated innate linguistic competence attached to the LTM. Once used in an utterance, they would be deposited in the more normally accessible area of the LTM through the internal monitor line and though initially weak would have made the first step toward becoming a part of the regularly stored retrievable data. Cumulative deposits would occur if the creolizing speaker used and/or heard them repeated also in the speech of others. Conflicting or alternative forms, as occurred with *chow chow* versus *kaikai* in Beche-la-mer in New Caledonia in the last century, could be evaluated and tagged on the basis of frequency, or of greater prestigiousness, but more likely on a more subtle and complex scale of overall suitability which would include, among other things, their similarity to already known items.

Input overload, on the other hand, would produce much more random false signals or distortions of existing ones. A number of comedians have based routines on the weird admixtures and distortions resulting from being confronted with competing inputs at the same time.

Results vary in the case of excess power according to the degree. Slightly more than normal power allows for the creative usages and coinages mentioned in Section 2.7, many of which only occur in passing, but others of which play a clear role in language change or in the elaboration which must accompany the functional expansion of language use into new domains. More excessive levels of power, as when the individual is ecstatic, nervous, or the like, result in wrong rule applications, inappropriate lexemes, phonetic mis-shaping, etc. This latter type would seem to play no significant role, however, in language change or development.

4. **Conclusion.** The first section of this paper dealt with certain issues apparently internal to pidgin and creole linguistics and attempted to show a larger unity between this subfield and sociolinguistics in general by demonstrating that pidgins and creoles, though distinct from other languages in some ways, are sociolinguistically indistinguishable from other types of

languages by dint of their adherence to common principles and processes. Sections 2 and 3 have illustrated how a single model of language acquisition/ performance can account for a great many observed phenomena relating to three separate but related areas of linguistic investigation—pidginization/ creolization of languages; L1/L2 acquisition; and the formation of non-native varieties of English. Though the model's ability to account for many observed or posited phenomena relating to these areas has been theoretically shown, much additional work and research are needed to test its applied adequacy.

ON THE GENESIS OF LANGUAGES
Mervyn C. Alleyne

I shall continue our focus on creole languages and try to give a critical evaluation of the papers presented earlier in this series, as well as of the general literature on the genesis of pidgins and creoles; and finally I will give my own interpretation of the genesis of these languages. It turns out that creole languages—three of them at least—are very interesting in that they represent perhaps the most recent examples of the genesis of new languages. The three to which I am referring are Saramaccan and Sranan (both spoken in Surinam) and Papiamentu (spoken in the Netherland Antilles). The reason why I say that the group of creole languages is interesting and that these creole languages are the most recent cases of the emergence of new languages is that, in looking at the emergence of new languages, we have to use not the names that are given to languages, which may respond to all kinds of needs and circumstances and which do not necessarily refer to the genesis of languages, but rather we have to use linguistic concepts of what a language is. In the perspective which I am taking here, it's going to be rather difficult to pinpoint the date of the emergence of what is called, say, Italian, because in this perspective Italian is really the unbroken continuation of Latin such that it is impossible to locate any point in the history of this continuity where one is able to say that the Italian language has emerged. That is to say that in the transmission of Latin in Western Europe there was a slow, imperceptible, continuous change that Latin was undergoing, such that no one generation felt, or was aware, that it was speaking a language different from that of any adjacent generation. From that point of view it is impossible to say where Italian begins and where Latin ends. So that in this particular case, we are not talking about the emergence of a new language at all, but of a continuation of Latin which has now acquired a new name. Also if you look at it in terms of the horizontal distribution of language in Western Europe, I am assuming (and this of course has to be empirically established) that in terms of the distribution of language over a geographical area it is impossible to say where the alleged entity called Italian begins and where another alleged entity called French begins and ends. In other words, if you move from the north of France right down into the boot of Italy, my assumption is that you will not cross a language frontier. That is, you cannot say that at this point, on one side of this line, Italian is spoken, and on the other side French is spoken. So that in this case also, to talk about the genesis of French or Italian is untenable. The most we can say is that there is a frontier somewhere on the Rhine; the language materials used by a monolingual speaker of "French" dialect on the west side of the Rhine belong to a different language from the language to which the materials used by a monolingual speaker on the east side belong.

In the case of the languages which I wish to discuss in this paper, there is absolutely no doubt, from whatever perspective one may look, that they emerged as new languages in the genetic sense, i.e. clear-cut language systems that are different from any other language systems either that might have preceded them in historical terms or with which they may be compared in horizontal terms. They also emerged at periods about which there is quite general agreement. People speak loosely about Papiamentu being Spanish-based or about Sranan being English- (or Portuguese-) based. The meaning of "based" in this usage is very imprecise and careless, and if we wish to be precise and careful, we should limit "based" to refer only to the origin of the major portion of the lexicon, i.e. the existence of cognate roots in the lexicon.

What obscures the issue with languages like Saramaccan or Sranan is that they are called creole languages, and one of the problems in creole language studies is to figure out precisely what "creole" means when we use the term in reference to language. Is "creole" an epithet of nationality as in the case of the French language when one refers to the language of the French nation? Of course this will not hold because there is no nation of people who are called *creole*. Is it a genetic term as Romance is or Germanic is, referring then to a language family which shares some common ancestor? Of course this has to be considered seriously as the reference for the term *creole* because these languages spoken around the globe are supposed to share certain structural features; but I don't think that anyone has proposed that all the languages commonly classified as creole go back to one unique ancestor, although we know that there is a claim that a substantial number of these languages go back to one common ancestor generally identified as a Portuguese pidgin. However, there are a number of other languages called creole for which the Portuguese pidgin has not been proposed as the ancestor so that although this notion of creole as a genetic term merits some examination, it is clear that it cannot easily refer to a genetic factor in the languages so designated. Another question to ask is whether or not *creole* is a typological term referring to a typological class of languages; but again this will not work because it has never been established that the particular structural features of creole languages constitute a unique class, typologically speaking. So we are left with a designation which is really something which we have inherited. That is, we have inherited a designation of a class of languages that goes back to the 19th century. Since then, a lot of interesting and very significant things have been said about these languages, but some of the basic definitions have persisted. Thus, at the recently held conference in St. Thomas on theoretical orientations in creole studies, it continued to be accepted that languages designated pidgin, creole, and postcreole have been involved in a well-defined developmental cycle and that there is a clear definitional process of reduction and/or expansion that typifies each stage in the development. In some cases, if a certain language had been designated a creole by the 19th-century classification, the task of 20th-century linguistics has been to attempt to establish the pidgin ancestry of the creole with all its definitional implications. However, there are not many clear cases where expansion has been established for creoles. It has been brilliantly inferred for Hawaiian and generalized to the Caribbean; there is currently a glorious opportunity to observe the process empirically for Melanesian although there do not seem to be any extraordinary changes taking place; but in a key creole like Saramaccan, which may represent the oldest layer of creole known to us, it fails to assert itself. You would expect to find in Saramaccan some—at least one piece—of the evidence of that pidgin stage which we assume to predate the development of Sranan, Jamaican, and indeed (if Bickerton is to be believed) Hawaiian. But alas it is not there. Everything typical of a creole structure that Jamaican or Sranan has is also there in Saramaccan, but the latter has a little more: vestiges of a noun class system which are slightly more vestigial than in Sranan and Jamaican, prenasalized stops, and distinctive lexical tone. And then there is Nigerian Pidgin English (and the other pidgins of West Africa) which is a pidgin in both name and function although structurally parallel to the expanded creoles of Africa and the Caribbean. This implies that a pidgin may expand and still remain a pidgin. Similarly, Guinea-Bissau *crioulo*, called Crioulo by its speakers, is still basically a pidgin: it has no native speakers, but it shows a closer similarity to Portuguese than, say, Haitian, a true creole, shows to French. This difference is presumably a result of considerable expansion in Haitian. Indeed, if we do believe in the pidgin-creole hypothesis, including the variant that maintains that creoles are relexifications of a Portuguese pidgin, it would be the pidgin-creoles of São Tomé, Guinea-Bissau, and Cape Verde that would establish this. As it is, no work supporting these hypotheses refers itself in any adequate way to the Portuguese-based dialects of West Africa.

Now I want to review the papers of this series and see how they relate to the question of creole languages and to consider how they fit or do not fit into the scheme which I support for the genesis of these languages. Let me say right here that in the scheme which I propose I attempt to deal with language form, language situations, and even language planning in the Caribbean. Studies of second language acquisition generally fail to be so general as to embrace all instances of second language acquisition. These are varied in circumstances, goals, processes, results; and we really need the most general framework within which all instances can be studied. What we do not need is a very limited experimentation that makes limited assumptions about goals and conditions and which then claims, either explicitly or implicitly, to be general. For example, Schumann, in discussing the genesis of a second language, i.e. the early stages of second language acquisition (which is of course of direct relevance to the emergence of pidgins and creoles), reports some very dubious goals, dubious, that is, insofar as they make general claims about second language acquisition. For example, Schumann presents the discourse perspective of Hatch in which it is claimed or hypothesized that "syntax is learned through conversation . . . [that] the learner's goal is to be able to engage in conversations with target language (TL) speakers. [The learner] wants to function in TL discourse and the acquisition of the TL syntax is the automatic by-product of learning to do so." This is in fact quite far from any experience of many second language acquirers, and in particular those second language acquirers who produced creole languages.

The next model presented by Schumann, that of Krashen, is more interesting in that it proposes a distinction between a learning system and an acquisition system. Learning involves the conscious incorporation of TL rules, and is facilitated by the explicit presentation of those rules coupled with feedback in the form of error correction. Acquisition, on the other hand, is the nonconscious incorporation of TL structures resulting from exposure to and interaction with TL speakers in genuine communicative contexts. He further contrasts, on the one hand, the child learner who begins by speaking some type of simple TL system with the input provided for the child keeping progressively just beyond the child's current stage of grammatical development, with, on the other hand, the adult learner who, not having time to develop an acquired competence with which to initiate TL speech, uses his native language as a substitute utterance initiator and produces TL words with native language syntax.

Thirdly, there is the neurofunctional model which claims three modes through which second language acquisition is directed:

1. *Monitor mode* which involves conscious application of learned grammatical rules to the production of TL utterances.
2. *Automation mode* which involves the nonconscious production of TL utterances through automated subroutines (i.e. prefabricated patterns, memorized chunks).
3. *Infrasystem mode* which involves the production of interlanguage utterances through task-specific neural constructs in the brain.

There is then an elaborate procedure whereby successive infrasystems are formed, each one giving way to a more advanced one, and with earlier infrasystems reemerging sometimes when the learner is fatigued, under pressure, or extremely relaxed.

There is finally the acculturation model of Schumann himself which maintains that second language acquisition is an aspect of acculturation and that a second language learner will acquire the TL only to the degree that he acculturates to the TL group.

First of all, we may dismiss the Hatch model as being totally inadequate. I will merely say here that the teleological behavior of language learners is crucial but is more complex than simply wishing to engage in conversation with TL speakers. One of the fascinating things about creole language formation is the extent to which there was an intention to limit conversation with TL speakers or rather to devise a medium which at the speaker's will could let in or shut out TL speakers. What I am hinting at here is that throughout the language history of Afro-Americans, including the period of the emergence or genesis of Western Hemisphere creole languages, interaction among Afro-Americans themselves—and in the early period this meant interaction among Africans of different ethnic origins—was more important for language development than interaction between Africans and TL speakers.

I go along with Krashen's distinction between learner and acquirer, but hasten to say that in a language acquisition situation both types may be represented, even in the same individual; and the phenomenon may be stated in terms of the different experiences of the TL gained by the same individual in different contexts or by different individuals or different groups in a language contact/language acquisition situation. I plan to say more about this later as it is fundamental to an understanding of the different types of creole languages which were generated in the Caribbean in different types of language situations. Again I stress that I am interested in the broadest framework that can accommodate all types of language acquisition/language learning phenomena, i.e. pidgins, creoles, decreolization, etc. Krashen's model seems to provide us also with the distinction between what are really the two models or theories of second language acquisition that are most generally accepted: the innate capacity theory and the behavioral theory.

What we may retain from the neurofunctional model is the notion of the successive infrasystems replacing each other and earlier ones reemerging when the learner is under fatigue or pressure. This matches very well what in creole studies is called "decreolization" or "expansion" that is agreed to take place whenever the creole exists in a language situation in which it is juxtaposed to an official language to which it is lexically related. A "continuum" of linguistic variation results, the precise nature of which is one of the current interests in creole and variation studies. The reemergence of earlier infrasystems may correspond to the movement of different speech acts up and down the continuum. And the psychological states referred to in the neurofunctional model do seem to generate some of the movement toward the extreme creole end of the continuum; but of course the movement responds to other factors as well which we shall have to consider.

Schumann seems to have presented a fourth model, the acculturation model, in which the first attempts at the acquisition of a second language are viewed as constituting pidginization. Schumann states that this model restricts itself to "natural second language acquisition that occurs under conditions of immigration to or extended sojourn in the TL country." If that is so, it immediately excludes itself as a model applicable to creole language genesis, since no case of a language designated a creole has emerged under these conditions. Yet it is important because we have here a suggestion that pidginization is common to all natural second language acquisition situations. I have agreed elsewhere that acculturation or its absence is a very important factor in accounting for different linguistic results in language contact situations, and I shall develop this further. For the moment, suffice it to say that I have proposed that it is very important to distinguish between those contacts where no acculturation takes place and those in which the limited interaction and communication between the groups in contact places a limited functional burden on the vehicle used for intergroup communication. This context would favor the emergence of a pidgin with both groups being involved in the process. In situations of settled contact where interaction is not occasional or among scattered individuals, the language input is very different. If there is some conscious simplification by both groups of the language agreed on to supply the input materials for the lingua franca, it is certainly the case that the full so-called "upper" language is used by its native speakers and heard by members of the other group(s). Secondly, as I shall attempt to show later, members of this latter group may see themselves obliged to undergo language shift because of the power situation in which they find themselves. The language shift that creates creole languages is not a qualitatively different case from other known instances of language shift. Certainly some of the special factors usually alluded to in creolization are different. Bickerton, for example, places considerable importance on the systematic separation of African slaves so that slaves belonging to the same ethnic and linguistic group would not find themselves on the same plantation. If this is meant, as it seems, to imply that the slaves were languishing in some preverbal state before they picked up something from a European language to express themselves, then this is quite false and absurd. The whole claim, by Schumann and others, that pidginization or universal-type simplification is involved in such situations and is the most important factor in language genesis in such situations does seem to imply the existence of some such preverbal stage. That is to say that in settled contacts, and in the specific case of the language contact in the Caribbean beginning from about the early 17th century, the claim seems to be that there was no full natural speech activity going on among Africans, and that whatever knowledge Africans had of their own languages somehow became suspended when they embarked on the acquisition of the other language in the contact situation. My claim of course is that this knowledge was there, was alive, and was actuated in considerable speech activity by Africans until this very day and was not suspended when Africans began to undergo language shift and language acquisition. It is important to note that bilingualism was already widespread in Africa and that many Africans coming to the New World were already competent in more than one African language. Furthermore, my claim is that the full European languages were heard, and that if any simplification occurred it was not as significant a factor as the transfer and continuity of the structure of the native languages in the acquisition of the other language. For example, the full inflectional system of French is to be found in fossilized form in French-based creoles; and English strong perfects are to be found copiously in English-based creoles, although they do not, of course, function there as "strong perfects."

Thus I would restrict pidginization processes to first language acquisition where the only knowledge possessed by the child is his innate mechanism, if such a mechanism does exist, and where universal-type simplification would be the most significant and perhaps the only factor that is operative; and I would also restrict these processes to language contact situations where no acculturation is taking place because the contact is occasional, seasonal, and among scattered individuals, thus placing a limited functional burden on the vehicle of communication adopted by persons involved in the contact.

Among the wide range of topics that are studied under the rubric of creole linguistics, the one which has attracted perhaps the most interest and attention is the genesis and early development of pidgins and creoles. There are virtually as many hypotheses as there are linguists, and these are the most ingenious and far-fetched theories. Unfortunately, a great deal of speculation has taken place, often with an unwillingness to delve too deeply into the contemporary facts and a readiness to pull uncorroborated statements out of the historical documentation of the social background and use them as support for linguistic hypotheses, all of which would make the historian or the traditional philologist shudder. Perhaps we are moving away from that kind of traditional, detailed research on the social and historical background which may be vital. Since the studies by Rens (1953) for Surinam and LePage and DeCamp (1960) for Jamaica, there has not been very much work along these lines. And the greatest gaps seem to be related to the Indian Ocean dialects to make quite sure, for example, that there is no historical connection between the Indian and the Atlantic Oceans, a connection which, by the way, does not require large-scale quantitative migration from Africa or the New World to the Indian Ocean to be significant linguistically. It seems to me that since we agree that pidgins and creoles demonstrate so forcefully the influence of social context on language change, language structure, and language usage, we should be concerned, if we wish to reconstruct the early language and language processes of pidgin and creole speakers, with reconstruction of the sociolinguistic situation at the time of its formation, with the structure of the communicative network, and the communicative needs of different sectors of the populations involved. Much, of course, is assumed, but many questions still remain to be researched and satisfactorily answered, such as distinguishing between those situations in which there was an equal exchange between two relatively homogeneous groups and those in which the exchange was more complex, both ethnolinguistically and in terms of pressures for developing new vehicles of communication. We should distinguish between those situations in which contact was irregular, seasonal, and among scattered individuals (like Hotel English for example) and those in which there were settled populations in continuous and relatively intense social interaction and where some kind of acculturation took place. In the case of the latter, it is vital to know precisely where the communicative pressures were felt most and what the structure of the communicative network was.

Beyond that, it seems to me that in tackling the problem of the genesis of these languages we should, in a logical, step-by-step progression, identify the factual and theoretical parameters of the question.

First: Did pidgins exist prior to the time we are considering them? In which case, were they transmitted virtually intact to their present speakers? Even the works which attempt to place *sabir* in the ancestry of some pidgins do not make this claim but rather, as I understand it, consider *sabir* as some kind of input or as one of the inputs into the situation. Nor can works which postulate, in the case of European language-based dialects, a specialized version of the European language (e.g. a nautical jargon or some sort of provincial dialect) as the ancestor of pidgins and creoles seriously claim that, say, Haitian Creole can be explained as resulting from the transmission of this specialized language on the territory of Haiti. We must accomplish these ends so that we may accept that the pidgins, in the form in which we are considering them, *emerged* at periods about which we are fairly well agreed and in localities and among populations which are not the subject of any great controversy.

Second: Did they emerge ex nihilo? This is really a very crucial point. I do not think that anyone will claim that there were no input language materials into the emergence of these languages. However, there is currently a most serious claim that some, I believe, of the semantic grammatical categories of the verb—and so far there is no explicit claim for anything else—emerged ex nihilo, i.e. without any linguistic input. This is to say that they were generated directly from new cognitive impulses experienced by the population and that they are different from the evolutionary changes that are imposed on a language by its speakers and their culture. I shall return to this later, but suffice it to say now that there is general agreement that there were linguistic inputs, both in terms of deep-structure semantic categories and in terms of surface forms. Even so, there is still the conceptual, in some sense philosophical, question as to whether "new" sociocultural phenomena are continuities with or without change or whether they are creations. This is not only a linguistic problem but one to which anthropology in general has addressed itself.

As a linguistic problem, it is related to another which I shall mention later concerning models or theories of language and language acquisition.

Third: Among whom did this emergence, these continuities or creations, take place? There is still some serious disagreement here. There is still some persistence, albeit diminished, in the belief that in the well-known cases which involve so-called "upper" and "lower" groups in contact, speakers of the upper language produced these forms. However, there is the contrary suggestion that speakers of the lower language have more compelling need for the development of new vehicles of communication. Compromise interpretations are also possible which would accept the notion that specialized forms of the upper language were one unit in the input materials (e.g. accepting the notion of a nautical jargon or some sort of provincial French) but that this underwent further changes in the process of being acquired by speakers of the lower language; or which would accept that there were new forms emerging among all speakers, but that what has come down to us as basic creole or basic pidgin are those forms which emerged among the lower speakers. We seem to need a clearer picture of the communicative networks and the communicative pressures in each individual case.

In addition to the foregoing, there is the question of whether we are dealing with language evolution or language acquisition. Whatever we believe about the above, it is quite clear that the lower groups in the case of the Atlantic and Indian Ocean creoles underwent language acquisition and language shift. Therefore, however we view emergence, we are dealing with language acquisition both as the major factor in the language changes that took place and as a precedent to any other evolutionary changes that the language might then later be embarking on. And it is very clear that it is at this point that the major theoretical questions arise. Are we to situate the emergence of our languages within a general theory of language contact and language acquisition, or are we to have recourse to a number of new ad hoc devices? Are all the a priori members of the a priori class necessarily to be accounted for within the same theoretical framework? Or do we try to see which ones can best be accounted for within the most general frameworks of language acquisition and language change, and which others need ad hoc devices? The great problem, of course, is that we do not yet have a generally accepted model for language acquisition. There is, as far as I know, no convincing definitive psycholinguistic research that allows us to choose definitively and conclusively between two major competitive theories of language acquisition: the behavioral theory and the cognitive theory. The behavioral theory emphasizes structural interference and transfer in the acquisition of a second language, whereas the cognitive theory stresses a developmental process with the apparently common innate grammars of speakers themselves working through common errors toward the acquisition of specific grammars of specific languages. The latter is more appropriately a theory of first language acquisition, and its adherents are seeking to apply these ideas to second language acquisition. These studies attempt to show that, for example, there is an invariant order of acquisition of forms and categories and an invariant order in the achievement of accuracy, based on some idea of degrees of complexity of forms and categories, in the acquisition of a first language. When applied to second language acquisition, this view would imply that the order of learning of the elements of the second language would be invariant, irrespective of the native language of the learner. We are thus now seeing the birth of very general so-called "pidginization hypotheses" for first language learning. On the other hand, other studies show variability in the acquisition, and this appears even more strongly in second language acquisition where there is absolutely no doubt that different native language speakers produce different kinds of orders of accuracy and, perhaps, acquisition in the learning process, even if we may not always be able to pinpoint precisely what features of the native language determine them.

The question is not merely whether a learner transfers features of his own language from a microtypological contrastive point of view, but whether the learner makes use of what he already knows, a strategy that affects all kinds of human activity and behavior. What a speaker already knows is grammar as an innate ability and (perhaps) mechanism, as well as his own specific native language grammar both as microfeatures and as globally generalized mechanisms for expressing semantic and grammatical values and relations, e.g. word order versus flexions, subordination versus coordination. This principle applies even to children learning their first language. Some psycholinguistic research on child second language acquisition shows that it applies there as well, and further psycholinguistic research suggests that, in children, temporal connectors that are learned early (like "before" or "after") and are interpreted as expressing a sequence of events identical in actual happening with the order of presentation in the sentence then influence the learning and interpretation of other temporal connectors, i.e. "while" and "until." For example, relative clauses will be interpreted in accordance with formulas and strategies learned earlier for simple sentences.

I must confess that I still do not understand rejection of the notion of interference or transfers, or, in terminology I prefer, continuities. They are so patent as to be incontrovertible, e.g. in the emergence of ethnic dialects of English in different parts of the world. In fact, I think the innate capacity theory is a gross non sequitur. The theory holds that humans, unlike animals, have some genetic endowment for language. We may or may not accept this. Nevertheless, until we have a few parents raise chimpanzees as their own children over a few generations, I will retain a little skepticism about that. But to go from there to conclude that humans inevitably need a specific-purpose learning device for language is also a gross non sequitur. An even grosser non sequitur is to say that general-purpose learning devices do not play a role in language acquisition but are in some strange way suspended when children or adults approach the learning of a language.

The solution which I would like to suggest, without being ideologically eclectic or middle of the road, is one that recognizes the validity of both conceptualizations and both theories, but identifies precisely in which areas each is significant. In first language learning, the innate capacity theory is strong, although even here the behavioral theory is still gathering support from research findings. Counter to the notion that children have some innate mechanism to construct a grammar out of the mass of unordered, unorganized material that they hear in the world around them, it is shown that in the parent-child communicative interaction there is, in fact, a great deal of teaching of well-formed grammatical structures by parents who repeat and complete the incomplete, ungrammatical utterances of children with fully accurate grammatical structuring. For second language acquisition, intuitively and on the basis of masses of evidence, continuity would have to be accorded, in my opinion, a preponderant role, leaving creativity to account for specific forms for which no input source is apparent. In dealing with the input source, we have to make allowances for plausible processes of change analogous to what in anthropology are called reinterpretations, remodelings, of such a nature and to such a degree that the relationship between the new form and the input source becomes difficult to decipher. It is the failure to make such allowances that reduces the merit of those statements that seek to refute the derivation by "substratomaniacs" of Atlantic creole verbal systems from generalized West African verbal systems, because the two do not match up exactly point by point.

The creativity concept also comes to us under the rubric of universals. There have been all sorts of ways in which these universals operate, from the simplistic universal simplification which takes isolated grammatical structures such as *he sick, me father house,* and even *de man cow,* as simplifications of *he's sick, my father's house,* and *bull,* up to the ingenious formulae which have speakers searching down not only into their own grammars but also into those of other speakers to select common, simple universal structures. And then, of course, there is the other hypothesis which explains the common, or should I say, the alleged common, verbal systems of Hawaiian and Atlantic by recourse to cognitive universals, which are always more interesting, although more difficult to handle than the statistical universal which looks at some languages, finds frequently occurring structures, dubs them universals, and then uses this notion of universal to account for their presence—a rather circular operation indeed. The weakness of the cognitive universal too is that it fails to establish any way, other than the existence of the linguistic forms themselves, for us to recognize these universal cognitive needs. Furthermore, even if we accept that human beings feel a strong cognitive compulsion to express aspect and tense inside the verb phrase (as I shall suggest later, this seems to be a common process in languages whereby lexical items progressively lose their semantic reference and become grammatical morphemes), that still does not explain the existence of common surface structures, or common orders of elements in the VP, or why the perfective, for example, should be expressed by zero.

The difficulty with "universals" is that the generally arbitrary nature of the linguistic sign places a restriction on the levels of grammatical organization that can be logically accepted as manifesting language universals. Thus, whereas it seems readily acceptable that tense-aspect should be a universally occurring element in human cognition and therefore would naturally turn up whenever speakers (particularly children) have to use their innate creativity to generate new language forms, there is nothing readily apparent in the neurological and cognitive systems of humans that makes it natural or inevitable that such semantic categories should be organized into perfective/nonperfective, habitual/progressive and with greater emphasis on these than on past/present/future, nor that these categories should be expressed by invariable particles preposed to the predicate. If it is argued that the use of invariable particles is merely the extension of an analytical syntax already existing in the pidgin and that the preposition responds to some implicational word order scheme (assuming that there are indeed such implicational relations in word order schemes), then there would still be a need to show why alone, of all the semantic categories, tense-aspect has to be thus accounted for (whereas the other categories are accounted for by transmission) and why the surface forms of tense-aspect should also be similar (perfective = zero; conditional = Past + Future). The question is all the more burning as there is a plausible way in which the tense-aspect categories of the VP can be seen as the result of transmission and continuity, i.e. these categories may still have to be accounted for by the input materials.

The other reasonably well-established versions of the universalist theory are less interesting for genesis and development studies, since whatever they may claim, they are really dealing with ways in which a structural typological relationship between pidgins and European languages may be stated. It is a pity that they make no attempts to consider a similar relationship between pidgins and West African languages, or Chinese, Malayo-Polynesian, Hawaiian, etc. The best statement of this version claims that pidgins, presumably those empirically observable and those inferred from the existence of current creoles, may possibly reveal in a more direct way than most natural languages the universal cognitive structures and processes that underlie all human language use. Pidgins are derivationally (in terms of the relationship between their deep and surface structures) shallower than natural languages and reflect universal deep (semantic) structure more directly than do natural languages. Natural language must of course be read here as European language. The use of universals here seems to be more in the nature of a descriptive statement based on the post-factum observation that all pidgins bear a certain relationship to language with which they happen to be compared at the time. Unlike the other version of universals mentioned earlier, this version does not have a clear role in accounting for the structure of pidgins in terms of genesis.

If indeed there is any implicit claim that pidgins and creoles derive their structures historically and genetically as a result of some universal process whereby speakers select deep structure forms (or derivationally shallow forms) of a language when they have to use it for certain restricted communicative purposes, it should be borne in mind that "deep structure" is not an exact replica of a property of the human brain, certainly not as a set of specific linear arrangements of grammatical formatives. It may be a reasonable way of representing some property of the brain which allows humans to generate language, but the specific grammar that generates a set of sentences and specifies their structure is not a replica of the brain. Everybody accepts this, I believe; but then we often inadvertently slip right back into concepts and statements that imply that a grammar is indeed a sentence factory, if indeed language is merely a set of sentences at all. We then have speakers doing all sorts of grammatical operations and processing what the grammar of their language does, as if the human mechanism for language is indeed the grammar. The question which we would then have to answer is whether particular speakers have standard theory grammars, relational grammars, equational grammars, corepresentational grammars, epiphenomenal grammars, panlectal grammars, or practice equi-deletion, X-bar derivations, or affix-hopping.

We also know that we must continually be careful not to confuse typological relationships with genetic relationships. Thus it can be shown, and it makes a fascinating study to show it, that the particular transitive predicate category empirically observable or reconstructable for Caribbean creoles which derives passives, intransitives, adjectival predicates, and adjectives reflects the deep structure of English which then requires a series of transformations to derive the surface forms such as *sicken, thicken,* plus whatever complex transformations are required to derive *be sick, be thick*; but this does not speak to an historical genetic derivation, but a certain kind of typological relationship. The study would be less fascinating, but perhaps more rewarding, if a similar comparative study were made between Caribbean dialects and some West African languages.

It is generally accepted that language change is a continually accelerating phenomenon in creole situations. From the earliest definitions, we have inherited the notion of reduction and expansion, and this was formalized in the different prefaces of the Hymes volume (1971), as well as elsewhere. One well-known attempt to demonstrate how expansion actually works in the pidgin-creole transition has not met with general approval. And indeed the grammaticization of lexical items—adverbs in the case I mentioned—bringing them into the Verb Phrase, unstressing them and making way for morphophonemic alternation which can then be exploited for stylistic purposes—all this is not really very unusual. It can be copiously documented for English or for Romance, and there are views that the Indo-European flexions are also to be explained by the grammaticization of lexical items. What is interesting and merits further examination is the same process of grammaticization, which is still apparently taking place, in Haitian in which a whole series of verbs are undergoing loss of stress, reduction, fixation in verbal auxiliary position, and are becoming less and less lexical semantic units and more and more grammatical units (*kapab, vini, fini, ge dwet*). And of course this is taking place at a time when one would expect the kind of expansion that has usually been associated with decreolization. It seems that we have not yet grasped precisely what takes place when a pidgin "expands" into a creole. As I said, the structure typical of Atlantic creoles can exist in a language which remains sociologically a pidgin; and the current transfer of Tok Pisin to sociological creole status is not being accompanied, or so it seems, by any considerable structural expansion. In Saramaccan, which must be considered to have become frozen relatively early, i.e. in the 17th century, there are a number of interesting variational patterns such as $kp \sim kw$, $nd \sim n$, and most interestingly *bari* 'to buy' which, unless it can be shown that Saramaccan speakers are now perceiving a correspondence between VV of their own speech and VCV of Sranan or Dutch, would have to be viewed as being modeled on the correspondence between V *liq* V of English and VV of their own speech. There *is* a clear rule of morpheme structure correspondence between English and Saramaccan, i.e. V *liq* V of English and VV of SM. Then *bari* would be a hypercorrect form showing that as early as we can reconstruct the beginning of Saramaccan, and therefore too of all Caribbean creoles based on English, a certain measure of remodeling in the direction of English was taking place. This of course seems to put the so-called "decreolization process" right back to the beginning and makes it really simultaneous with the so-called "creolization process" and with the so-called "pidginization process" (since in the 17th century, Saramaccan would have been just emerging from its pidgin status)—all of which **seem** to me, although the logical links cannot be established at length here, to point to the need for viewing these creoles at least as products of quite normal language development in contact situations, or else viewing all language development in contact situations as being inherently and potentially creolizing and decreolizing.

I am claiming then that the development cycle of pidgin → creole → post-creole characterized by reduction in the pidgin stage followed by continuous expansion into the creole and postcreole stages has not been established, and that, certainly for the Caribbean, a general framework of language contact producing different kinds of language change arising out of different experiences of language contact can account for all types of language phenomena, including language situations and language planning programs.

To understand the framework which I am proposing, it is very interesting to look at Caribbean language situations. They represent the full typology of such situations: bilingualism, diglossia, continuum, monolingualism. These different types of language situations are presented as a typology—a full one—of language situations, but in fact they are really idealized points that we have come to isolate on a continuum of shift from a situation of maximally discrete linguistic systems in coexistence (bilingualism) to one of a maximally homogeneous system in monolingualism. Beginning with bilingualism, i.e. the contact of discrete systems, we may get the development of grades of inter-language phenomena (infrasystems?) which may, as in the case of the Carib-bean, become crystallized or frozen, producing diglossia, i.e. preserving one language which is the upper language and another which is the crystallization of the interlanguage phenomena. The latter phenomenon will show clear vocabulary relationships with the upper language but will reveal a syntax and phonology quite different from those of the upper language. Therefore, we have a diglossia situation with two codes showing similarities on one level of structure (lexicon) and which come to exist in complementary distribution in the way in which they function in the communicative network. What also happens is that, as a result of the crystallization of interlanguage phenomena, there is the possibility of a new language emerging (as in the case of Sranan, Saramaccan, Papiamentu) when the upper language in the contact situation disappears for whatever reason (in the cases cited above, there was a change in colonial power) and all that is left of the original contact situation is the interlanguage which is frozen and no longer susceptible to any changes through the influence of the upper language. But in another case where the upper language is preserved and where different groups, as I said earlier, have different experiences of contact, variable language forms develop that can be measured or interpreted in terms of different degrees of deviancy from the norm of that upper language.

As far as different experiences of contact are concerned, in the case of Caribbean plantations, there was an occupational stratification among slaves which correlated with degrees of contact with European culture and language. Domestic slaves, for example, had much closer contact and interaction with Europeans and had a different experience of language acquisition. They developed certain language styles which separated them from the field slaves who formed the bulk of the slave population and who were farthest removed from contact with European culture. Then we have a middle group of drivers and artisans, the former being working gang leaders who had to develop quite complex communicative skills because, for example, they received messages from the European masters which then had to be transmitted by them to the field slaves. In cases where the upper language remained in contact, different experiences of contact resulted in the development of different language phenomena, which really means that as early as the very beginning of the contact situations a continuum of linguistic variation emerged, repre-sented by different groups having different experiences of contact and pro-ducing different kinds of language forms as a result. Field slaves developed forms of language which represented a maximum degree of deviancy from the

European norm, which then went through driver/artisans and domestics and finally into speakers of the European language. This then is the basis of the existence of the current continuum situations. The post-emancipation period in areas like Jamaica and Guyana further accentuated the continuum structure of language variation.

Cases where diglossia exists (e.g. Haiti) are cases where the sociological conditions of the contact situation did not produce a large number of representatives of the group of drivers/artisans and domestics but where there was a great predominance of field slaves, and where, in the post-emancipation period, social developments did not produce a large number of people involved in social mobility. There is then little movement of people on the social scale and correspondingly little movement on the linguistic scale. So we have the appearance of a structural gap between two language systems and a great deal of controversy as to whether this structural gap actually exists. Politically speaking, there is a movement in Haiti to assert the existence of such a structural gap because the existence of such a gap places Haitian Creole in a certain kind of relationship with French. Haitian Creole can then be asserted as a completely independent language system and focused on for the purpose of expressing a distinct Haitian national identity. But it is clear, and a few writers have alluded to it, that there are intermediate forms in Haiti parallel to the kind of intermediate forms that help to constitute the continuum of Jamaica and Guyana. The difference is that in the case of Haiti the people who use these intermediate forms are very few because of the socioeconomic situation of Haiti, whereas in the case of Jamaica, the vast majority of speakers habitually use the intermediate forms, and there are now few speakers situated at the extreme creole pole of the continuum.

The difference, then, between the early situation in Jamaica and the current one is not so much, as some may think, in the new emergence of "postcreole" forms out of an earlier discrete English language versus creole situation, but rather a new movement in the demographic importance of these intermediate forms. My claim therefore is that the postcreole continuum, as a set of linguistic relationships between forms, existed from the very inception of the contact situation, but that today intermediate forms have greater demographic value and greater recognition than they had at the beginning.

The other significant thing that has happened to the Jamaican continuum is that, as you go through the centuries, the extreme creole end is constantly losing forms, i.e. forms are constantly being lopped off from this end. For example, forms typical of Saramaccan or Sranan, such as vowel final syllables, have virtually disappeared from Jamaican and exist only in relic form or in archaisms. By and large, Jamaican has moved closer to the English syllabic structure, but of course not completely. A very general morpheme structure rule for Saramaccan or Sranan adds a vowel to every syllable which in the English lexical base ends in a consonant. But in Jamaican there are now only about half a dozen of such cases, and they are becoming quite archaic (*luku* 'look', *rata* 'rat', *yeri* 'hear').

In the case of Barbados and other areas which now have monolingualism, we have copious evidence that in the 19th century there was a form of speech akin to Sranan or Jamaican. This means that certain socioeconomic conditions existing there have caused the complete disappearance of the extreme creole end (although a very small number of relics still exist) as well as the disappearance of the intermediate varieties such as exist in Jamaican. All we have in Barbados now is a kind of orthodox monolingual situation which displays variation between standard and nonstandard forms. The framework which I am trying to develop here would account, then, not only for incontrovertibly new languages such as Sranan but also for controversial continuum situations or diglossia situations such as exist in Haiti, as well as the noncontroversial continuum of Jamaica and the monolingualism of Barbados.

In conclusion, as far as language planning is concerned, it will be found that in cases where the interlanguage froze and the upper language disappeared (Sranan, Papiamentu), the creoles enjoy the greatest prestige. There is a correlation between the degree of prestige which a creole language enjoys and the language situation in which it exists. Where new, completely autonomous language systems emerged, there is the possibility that speakers could focus on them as independent languages and develop positive attitudes toward them. Then, too, there is a tendency for these languages to embark on standardization processes by which they will become "languages" in the sense of being codified and used in official domains. The presence in Haiti of two language systems which share a level of structure in common creates some difficulty for Haitians in focusing on Haitian Creole as an independent language. There is still considerable debate in Haiti as to whether the orthography for Haitian Creole should be a gallicizing one based on French spelling or whether it should be a completely phonemic and independent orthography. When we come to Jamaica, we find that there is no movement for the elevation of Jamaican Creole to a higher status and that no one is concerned with orthography or standardization.

THE DEVELOPING COMPLEMENTIZER SYSTEM OF TOK PISIN: SYNTACTIC CHANGE IN PROGRESS[1]

Ellen Woolford

1. Introduction

Tok Pisin is the major lingua franca of Papua New Guinea. It originated as a pidgin, but it now has more than 10,000 young native speakers (Sankoff and Laberge 1973). Because these native speakers comprise less than 5 percent of the total number of Tok Pisin speakers and because the language of these native speakers differs little from that of their parents (Sankoff and Laberge 1973), it is difficult to say whether Tok Pisin is currently a pidgin or a creole. Todd (1974) classifies it as an extended pidgin, and it could also be called an incipient creole.

The question of whether the changes that are occurring in Tok Pisin during this transition period from pidgin to creole are unique to creolization or whether they can be identified as ordinary processes of language change is of major interest. The claim will be made here that the mechanism of change by which Tok Pisin is developing a complementizer system is a quite ordinary process of language change, namely, syntactic reanalysis. No special processes unique to creolization are involved.[2] If Tok Pisin can be said to be undergoing creolization, then creolization is governed by the same principles that govern other language change. If there does exist some unique kind of language change that should be set apart by the label "creolization," it is the case argued for by Bickerton (1975). According to Bickerton, in situations where children do not have sufficient input from any existing language to learn it as their native language, the children create a new language out of the fragments of the languages they hear plus their knowledge of universal grammar. This case will not be considered here.

In a case such as Tok Pisin in which a stable pidgin is created before native speakers are acquired,[3] the only difference between creolization and other language change (besides, perhaps, the rate of change) is that the normal balance between changes that lead to simplification of the grammar and changes that lead to increased grammatical complexity is upset. The net result is increasing elaboration of the grammar. (See Bever and Langendoen 1972 on the normal balance of language change.)

The rapid, ongoing change in Tok Pisin gives us an unusual chance to study syntactic change in progress. From the investigation of the Tok Pisin complementizer system that follows, it is concluded that, at least in this case, the progress of syntactic change is not unlike that described by Labov and others for sound change. (See Weinreich, Labov and Herzog 1968 and Labov 1972.) What appears to be abrupt and discontinuous change in an historical perspective is shown, after close examination of the change in progress, to be a smooth progression of small steps joined by the mortar of variation and ambiguity.

If we could look back on the present from several hundred years hence, it might appear that a new phrase structure rule, $\bar{S} \rightarrow$ COMP S, had suddenly been added to the grammar of Tok Pisin. What we see now, however, is a period in which two grammatical systems coexist. This is made possible by the fact that the two different grammatical systems can produce the same surface strings. Thus, during the transition period, the underlying structure of complement sentences in Tok Pisin is ambiguous. The new system comes in gradually by means of step-by-step changes in the lexicon. Individual speakers vary a great deal with respect to which verbs in their lexicons are marked to take the new type of complement.

This process by which syntactic change can occur gradually, without any gap in communication, is called syntactic reanalysis. Langacker (1977) describes syntactic reanalysis as a process in which a sentence is reanalyzed by some language learners as having a different underlying structure. This reanalysis of the underlying structure does not produce any immediate change in the surface string, and thus communication is not impaired. Later, however, subsequent changes have surface structure consequences that resolve the ambiguity and verify that reanalysis has occurred.

Three different instances of syntactic reanalysis in Tok Pisin have created three different complementizers: one from a general preposition, *long* 'to, of, for, etc.'; one from an adverb, *olsem* 'thusly'; and one from a conjunction, *na* 'and'. In their original roles as prepositions and adverbs, these words appear in positions just preceding complement clauses. Since we are observing changes in progress, some speakers still use these words in their original capacity; others have reanalyzed them as complementizers. Because such ambiguity is a necessary part of the change process, it is very difficult for the linguist to find hard evidence that reanalysis has actually occurred in any particular sentence. Nevertheless, there is evidence which, although not entirely conclusive, indicates that syntactic reanalysis is in progress in Tok Pisin and a complementizer system is being created.

In the absence of movement rules in Tok Pisin that might provide syntactic tests that would clearly indicate the correct underlying structure of particular sentences,[4] the best evidence available that Tok Pisin now has $\overline{S}$-type complements and complementizers is the following: A grammatical system that includes $\overline{S}$-type complements and complementizers predicts the actual behavior of *long, olsem,* and *na* much better than does a system without them. Moreover, a fourth complementizer, *we,* has recently begun to appear in a surface position that did not exist in Tok Pisin before the $\overline{S}$ structure was introduced. In Sections 2 through 5, the details of the behavior of *long, olsem, na,* and *we* will be presented, and the old and the new complementation systems will be laid out and contrasted. Evidence and argumentation will be given to support the hypothesis that Tok Pisin is developing a complementizer system by the mechanism of syntactic reanalysis and that that system has the following properties:

A. In the lexicon, verbs can be subcategorized to take one of three complement types: $_{PP}[P\ S]$, $_{\overline{S}}[COMP\ S]$, and S.[5]

B. There is no subcategorization for particular complementizers. COMP may be filled by any one of the complementizers—*long, olsem,* or *na*—in VP complements and by *we* in relative clauses.

C. There is an optional rule of complementizer deletion. The frequency of application of this rule increases with decreasing age of the speaker and with increasingly urban environments.

This system correctly predicts the following facts about Tok Pisin:

1. *Long* is obligatorily present before the complement clauses of certain verbs, but *olsem, na,* and *we* are never obligatory.

This is predicted by the fact that prepositions are not deletable, but complementizers are. When *long* is a preposition, it is obligatorily present; but when it is a complementizer, it is optional. The deletability of *long* is determined by the preceding verb because the selection for PP or $\overline{S}$ complements is marked on individual verbs in the lexicon.

2. If *long* is not obligatory, then *long, olsem,* and *na* are interchangeable.

This is predicted by the fact that if the structure of the complement is $_{\overline{S}}[COMP\ S]$, any one of the complementizers may be chosen to fill the complementizer slot (except the relative clause complementizer *we*). If, on the other hand, the structure of the complement is $_{PP}[P\ S]$, then only the preposition *long* may appear, and as a preposition it is obligatory.

3. There is a great deal of variation among individual speakers as to which verbs take which complement types.

This is predicted if verbs are subcategorized in the lexicon for complement type because things marked in the lexicon are notoriously variable among speakers.

2. Long

Long is a general-purpose preposition in Tok Pisin, and it has a wide variety of meanings in different contexts. Some of these are illustrated in the following examples:

(1) *Long* moning ol i paitim garamut.
     In the morning they beat the drum.
(2) Yupela i go antap *long* ples.
     You (pl.) go up *to* the village.
(3) Yumitupela sindaun *long* dispela arere *long* wara.
     we (incl.) (dual) sit *on* this side *of* river
     Lets sit on the river bank.
(4) Yu ken i kam bek gen *long* lukim mipela.
     you can come back again *for* see us
     You can come back again (for) to visit us.
(5) Nogat stori *long* toki m yu.
     (neg.) have story *for* tell you
     (I) have no stories (for) to tell you.

I will argue that Tok Pisin has a phrase structure rule that expands or rewrites PP as either P NP or P S. (A similar claim has been made for English by Emonds 1976 and others.) Examples (1) through (3) above have prepositional phrases of the $_{PP}$[P NP] type, whereas examples (4) and (5) have prepositional phrases of the $_{PP}$[P S] type. Prepositions can never be deleted in either construction.

Besides the purpose clauses in examples (4) and (5), there are certain verbs whose sentential complements must always be preceded by *long*:

(6) Mi amamas *long* bekim pas yu bin raitim long mi bipo.
     I am pleased (*for*) to answer the letter you wrote to me before.
(7) Tambu tru *long* stil, bipo.
     taboo real *for* steal before
     It was absolutely taboo (*for*) to steal before.

In contrast to these verbs, there is another set of verbs whose complement clauses are only optionally preceded by *long* for most speakers:

(8a) I no inap *long* baibai yumi ken bekim bek.
     (neg.) possible *for* (Fut.) we can repay back
     It is not possible that we will be able to repay it.
(8b) Bifo i no inap man i stil *olsem.*
     before (neg.) possible person steal *thus*
     Before, it was not possible for people to steal like that.
(9a) Ol i no save *long* ol i mekim singsing.
     they (neg.) know *that* they make ritual
     They did not know that they had performed a ritual.
(9b) Ol i no save samting bai kukim ol.
     they (neg.) know thing (Fut.) burn them
     They did not know the thing would burn them.

I claim that complements obligatorily preceded by *long* have the structure $_{PP}$[P S], whereas complements only optionally preceded by *long* have the structure $_{\overline{S}}$[COMP S].

A longitudinal study of the frequency of *long* deletion before complement clauses indicates that the possibility of deleting *long* in this context is a recent development. Consider the verb *inap* 'possible' or 'able' since it occurs more frequently with complements than other verbs in the data. From the texts in Hall (1943) we find that all complement clauses of *inap* are preceded by *long*, but unfortunately there were only two such complements in the data. It is a problem to find any clauses strung together in the earlier data because people tended to confine themselves to simple sentences, especially in narrative. Nevertheless, the hypothesis that previously all complements of *inap* had to be preceded by *long* is supported by data on contemporary speakers. In the data that I collected in 1975, there is a definite correlation between increasing age and a greater percentage of complements of *inap* preceded by *long*.[6] This correlation is shown in Table 1 (page 113).

It appears that, prior to World War II, all complement clauses had the structure $_{PP}$[P S] as in (10):

(10)
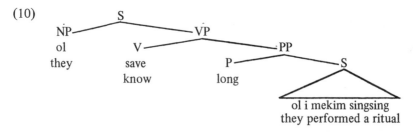

TABLE 1

Percentage of Complement Clauses of the Verb *inap* 'possible, able' That Are Preceded By *long* in Data Collected in Papua New Guinea in 1975

Speaker	Sex	Area of Origin[7]	Age	Percent Occurrence of *long/inap* ___ S	Actual Count
S.	male	Bogia (Madang)	22	0	0/4
J.	male	Finschhafen	20	0	0/5
K.	female	Chimbu	21	4	1/24
L.	female	Wabag & Kainantu	35-40	37	21/56
P.	female	Pindiu	35-40	67	4/6
G.	male	Sepik	50	83	10/12
F.	male	Finschhafen	45-50	86	12/14

At some point in time following World War II, language learners began to reanalyze sentences like (10) as having the structure in (11):

(11)
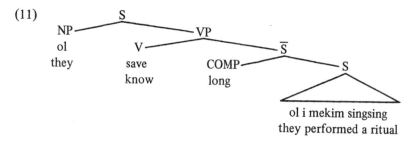

This reanalysis resulted in the addition of a phrase structure rule, $\bar{S} \rightarrow$ COMP S, to the grammar. Subsequently, a rule of complementizer deletion, COMP $\rightarrow \emptyset$, was also added to the grammar, and the difference between the underlying PP and $\bar{S}$ structures became detectable on the surface.

At the present time, there is a set of verbs that are still subcategorized by all speakers to take $_{PP}$[P S] complements. Two of these were given in examples (6) and (7). There is also a class of verbs that are subcategorized to take $_{\bar{S}}$[COMP S] complements by all speakers. Sentences (8) and (9) were examples of this class. In between these two poles, however, there is a large group of verbs that are subcategorized to take different complements by different speakers. This is what we expect in any situation where change is in progress. If the choice of complement type is specified in the lexical entries of individual verbs (as it is in English, cf. Grimshaw 1979), it is not surprising that the substitution of $\bar{S}$ complements for PP complements should proceed through the lexical system at different rates for different speakers.

Despite this great amount of variation in the speech community, individuals may have fairly simple and regular grammars. For example, let us consider the three speakers in Table 2 (page 115) who have very different frequencies for the occurrence of *long* preceding the complements of different verbs.

This sort of variation among speakers is just what we would predict if these speakers had the lexical subcategorization for complement types as in Table 3 (page 115). Verbs such as *laik* 'want [intransitive]' whose complements have never been preceded by *long,* either in the old data from Hall (1943) or in the recent data, are subcategorized to take bare S complements.[8] Verbs such as *laikim* 'want [transitive]' are still subcategorized to take bare S complements by the oldest speakers, but they are now being changed to

TABLE 2

Speaker	Age	Percent Use of *long* Preceding the Complements of:			
		laik 'want' (intr.)	*laikim* 'want' (trans.)	*giaman* 'pretend'	*tokim* 'tell'
G.	50	0 (0/17)	0 (0/4)	100 (3/3)	50 (1/2)
P.	35-40	0 (0/13)	100 (1/1)	100 (1/1)	50 (1/2)
K.	21	0 (0/53)	0 (0/2)	0 (0/5)	0 (0/3)

TABLE 3

G. (Age 50)	P. (Age 35-40)	K. (Age 21)
laik [___ S]	*laik* [___S]	*laik* [___S]
laikim [___S]	*laikim* [___P S]	*laikim* [___$\overline{\text{S}}$]
giaman [___P S]	*giaman* [___P S]	*giaman* [___$\overline{\text{S}}$]
tokim [___$\overline{\text{S}}$]	*tokim* [___$\overline{\text{S}}$]	*tokim* [___$\overline{\text{S}}$]

take more complex complements by younger speakers.[9] If the small number of tokens represented in Table 2 is at all representative, there seems to be an implicational progression such that a verb is subcategorized to take a $_{pp}$[P S] complement before it is subcategorized to take an $_{\overline{S}}$[COMP S] complement. This is additional support for the hypothesis that the $\overline{S}$ complement is created by syntactic reanalysis of the $_{pp}$[P S] complement.

The only thing that needs to be added to this system to completely predict the pattern of variation in Tok Pisin speakers' use of *long* preceding complement clauses is a variable rule of COMP deletion. As we saw in Table 1, complementizer deletion correlates with the speaker's age and probably with the rural-urban continuum.

In the introduction to this paper, it was mentioned that since the process of syntactic reanalysis necessarily involves structural ambiguity, it is difficult to prove that reanalysis has actually taken place. Considering the evidence presented up to this point, one might argue that a seemingly simpler model that does not involve syntactic reanalysis at all fits the facts as well as this one does. One might argue that Tok Pisin never had a $_{pp}$[P S] complement type at all. Suppose, instead, that Tok Pisin has always had the choice of subcategorizing verbs to take either S or $\overline{S}$ complements and that the only changes that have occurred are the introduction of a variable rule of complementizer deletion and a change in the subcategorization of some verbs to take $\overline{S}$ instead of S complements. Under this model, all the verbs in Table 3 that are subcategorized to take P S complements would be subcategorized to take $\overline{S}$ complements, but they would be marked to indicate that the variable rule of complementizer deletion could not apply to them.

Evidence supporting the original model involving a $_{pp}$[P S] complement type will be presented at the end of Section 3 on the behavior of the complementizer *olsem*.

3. *Olsem*

Olsem has a wide variety of functions and meanings in Tok Pisin. Some of these are illustrated in the following examples:

(12) Em i kamap yangpela boi *olsem* James.
      he grow young boy *like* James
      He grew up to be a young boy *like* James (i.e., James' size).
(13) Na insait long bus i nogat ol *olsem* ol pikinini bilong diwai nabaut na
      olsem laulau?
      and inside of forest (pl.) *like* (pl.) child of tree around and *like* Malay
      apples

And in the forest weren't there *like*[10] fruit of trees around and *like* Malay apples?

(14) Em i go i stap *olsem* wan mun samting.
he go stay *like* one month approximately
He went and stayed about one month.

(15) Binatan tasol i mekim nais *olsem*.
insects only vibrate *thus*
It was just insects that were vibrating *like that*.

(16) *Olsem* nau bai yumi tok wanem?
thus now (Fut.) we say what
So now what will we say?

(17) Em tingting em behain bai *olsem* yet.
he think it later (Fut.) *same* still
He thinks it will still be the *same* in the future.

(18) "Yu lukaut," em i tokim mi *olsem*.
"You watch out," he said to me *thusly*.

(19) Elizabeth i tok *olsem*, "Yumi mas kisim ol samting pastaim."
Elizabeth spoke thusly, "We must get things first."

(20) Yu no ken ting *olsem* mipela i lusim tingting long yu pinis.
you (neg.) can think *thusly/that* we lose thought of you complete
You must not think *like/that* we have forgotten you.

In example (20), *olsem* as an adverb is in position to be reanalyzed as a complementizer. This sentence could have either of the following underlying structures (ignoring the negative and modal):

(21)

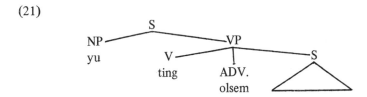

(22)

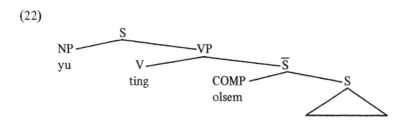

In example (23) from a young urban speaker, it is fairly clear from the intonation that *olsem* is being used as a complementizer:

(23) Na yupela i no save *olsem* em i matmat?
       and you (pl.) (neg.) know *that* it cemetery
       And you did not know *that* it was a cemetery?

The use of *olsem* as a complementizer is quite similar to the use of *that* as a complementizer in English, but it is unlikely that borrowing was involved. More likely, the similarity arises from a similarity of origin. Although there is no actual documentation for this process in Old English, it is generally assumed that the demonstrative ð̂aet was reanalyzed as a complementizer (Lehmann 1972 and Allen 1977) in much the same way that *olsem* was reanalyzed in Tok Pisin as in the following example from Allen (1977:126):

(24a) "John left." He said that.
(24b) He said that: "John left."
(24c) He said that John left.

There is a very similar phenomenon in Buang (a New Guinean language spoken near Lae) mentioned in Sankoff's article in this volume. Buang *(na)be* behaves much like Tok Pisin *olsem. (Na)be* is used as: 1) an adverb meaning 'thus' or 'like that'; 2) as an introducer of direct speech; and 3) as a complementizer. Nevertheless, Buang *(na)be* should not be considered to be the source of the Tok Pisin complementizer *olsem* for the reasons given by Sankoff (this volume) concerning the source of *ia* and because of the lack of any phonological similarity between *olsem* and *(na)be.*

The reanalysis of a lexical item that precedes a direct quote as a complementizer is apparently a fairly common occurrence in language change. Lord (1976) lists a large number of languages including the Kwa languages and other African and Asian languages that have complementizers identical to or virtually identical to the verb meaning *say* in those languages. She presents detailed arguments for the case in Ewe, including the fact that *bé* 'say' has lost semantic, syntactic, and morphological properties of the verb in its role as a complementizer. One example of the sort of structurally ambiguous string that led to reanalysis of *bé* as a complementizer in Ewe is in (25), taken from Lord (1976:182):

(25) fia—gbé—bé—wómagàvá—o
      chief—refuse (say)—∅—they-PRON-come—NEG
      The chief refused, said they should not come.
      The chief forbade that they should come.

Further evidence that *olsem* has been reanalyzed as a complementizer in Tok Pisin comes from the fact that there is phonological reduction of *olsem* to *olse* and even to *se* for some speakers. Mühlhäusler (forthcoming) gives examples of *se* introducing indirect speech, although he has found it only after the verbs *ting* 'think' and *tok* 'say'.

Let us now return to the question raised at the end of Section 2. Does the grammar of Tok Pisin allow a choice of three complement types—S, PP, and $\bar{S}$ (the third one being a recent innovation)—or does the grammar have only two complement types—S and $\bar{S}$? Although one might favor the two-choice model on the grounds of its simplicity, it turns out that this model leaves many facts unexplained and requires some arbitrary stipulations.

The two-choice model predicts that when verbs are subcategorized to take $\bar{S}$-type complements, any one of the complementizers should be able to fill the COMP slot. Nevertheless, an attempt to substitute *olsem* for *long* in sentences such as (6) and (7) fails, as we see in examples (26) and (27) below:

(26) *Mi amamas olsem bekim pas yu bin raitim long mi bipo.
      I am pleased that (I) answer the letter you wrote to me before.
(27) *Tambu tru olsem stil, bipo.
      It was absolutely forbidden that (one) steal before.

In contrast, the three-choice model predicts that there will be some complements—the $_{PP}$[P S] variety—in which only *long* may precede the complement clause. Moreover, the three-choice model correctly predicts that in just those cases, *long* cannot be deleted.

The two-choice model could be shored up with a means of subcategorizing for specific complementizers and a means of specifying that complementizers following certain verbs are exempt from the COMP deletion rule. Nevertheless, it would remain an unexplained accident that the set of verbs that are subcategorized to take *long* is precisely the same set of verbs whose complements are exempt from the COMP deletion rule. There are no instances of COMP nodes that must simply be filled by any complementizer.

The three-choice model also correctly predicts that whenever *long* is optional in a complement, the complement is an $\overline{S}$-type complement and *olsem* can fill the COMP slot as well as *long* can, e.g. in sentences (8) and (9) the substitution of *olsem* for *long* is perfectly grammatical, cf. (28) and (29):

(28) I no inap olsem baibai yumi ken bekim bek.
      It is not possible that we will be able to repay it.
(29) Ol i no save olsem samting bai kukim ol.
      They did not know that the thing would burn them.

4. *Na*

Na 'and' in Tok Pisin is an ordinary coordinate conjunction that joins words, phrases, or sentences, just as *and* does in English. Since *na* appears in a position just preceding clauses, it is also in a position to be reanalyzed as a complementizer.

(30) Husat tokim yu *na* yu kam?
      who told you *and* you come
      Who told you to come?
(31) Ol papamama na ol hetman i mas tok *na* ol i marit.
      (pl.) parent and (pl.) elder must say *and* they marry
      The parents and elders must tell them to get married.
                                            (Mühlhäusler forthcoming)

Unlike the case of *long* and *olsem,* the reanalysis of *na* as a complementizer actually changes the meaning slightly in some sentences, and this makes it possible to find examples in which *na* must be a complementizer instead of a conjunction. If the clauses in (32) were merely conjoined, the sentence would make no sense:

(32) Gutpela *na* yu kam.
      good *and* you come
      It is good *that* you come.

5. *We*

The three complementizers discussed so far only appear in complements in the verb phrase. They are never used in $\bar{S}$ constructions in relative clauses. A separate complementizer, *we,* is used by a very small percentage of Tok Pisin speakers, but only in relative clauses.[11] As are the other Tok Pisin complementizers, *we* is always optional.

Although there is no separation between relative clause complementizers and other complementizers in modern English, this may be the exceptional case. Besides Tok Pisin, both Irish and Biblical Hebrew have separate complementizers for relative clauses,[12] and this was the case in Old English as well (Allen 1977:139). It is highly probable that relative clause complementizers and VP complement complementizers always enter languages by separate routes, although they may later merge as they have done in English.

Elsewhere in the grammar of Tok Pisin, *we* is used as the *wh*-word 'where' by all speakers, as in (33):

(33) Dispela tupela man i stap *we*?
      this two man be located where
      Where are those two men?

As a complementizer, *we* is simply generated in COMP position in relative clauses, and there are no obvious intermediate steps by which this change came about.

(34) Dispela man i kolim stret man *we* em i poisinim long en.
      this man name exact man *that* he did-black-magic on him
      This man named precisely the man *that* (he) performed black magic on him.
(35) Mipela ol *we* i save kaikai saksak em i putim long mipela tasol.
      we (pl.) *that* know eat sago he put to us only
      We *who* are used to eating sago, they gave it to us only.

It cannot be argued that *we* gets into the COMP node by *wh*-movement because Tok Pisin relatives have resumptive pronouns which occupy the site from which *we* would have been moved.[13] Moreover, I have presented extensive arguments in earlier work (Woolford 1978a and 1978b) that Tok Pisin has no rule of *wh*-movement. Finally, there is evidence that *we* in this context is a complementizer and not a *wh*-word because it loses the semantic information that it carries as the *wh*-word 'where'. In both examples (34) and (35), *we* has lost all of its locative meaning and is being used with human subjects.

Although *we* did not become a complementizer by the process of syntactic reanalysis as in the case of *long, olsem,* and *na,* these previous instances of syntactic reanalysis established the $\overline{S}$ structure and the COMP node. This created a place for *we* to be generated where none had existed previously.

6. Conclusion

The data that have been presented in Sections 2 through 5 fit well with the hypothesis that Tok Pisin has developed a complementizer system by the process of syntactic reanalysis. A preposition, an adverb, and a conjunction occurring in positions immediately preceding complement clauses have been reanalyzed as complementizers. As a result, a new phrase structure rule, $\overline{S} \rightarrow$ COMP S, has been added to the grammar. Once this $\overline{S}$ construction was added, a relative clause complementizer appeared in a position that did not previously exist, i.e. the COMP node.

The $\overline{S}$-type complement is slowly spreading through the verb system as more and more verbs are subcategorized in the lexicon to take this new type of complement. In addition to the variation produced by differences in verb subcategorization for complement type in different speakers, further variation is produced by a variable rule of complementizer deletion. Complementizer deletion is increasing rapidly in younger speakers and in urban areas.

All the changes involved in the development of a complementizer system in Tok Pisin are quite ordinary processes of language change. There is nothing involved that is unique to creolization.

NOTES

1. This research was supported in part by NIMH Fellowship No. 5F32 MHO7244-02. I would like to thank Derek Bickerton, Joan Bresnan, John McCarthy, Norm Mundhenk, Pieter Muysken, Haj Ross, Gillian Sankoff, and William Washabaugh for valuable comments and discussions. I would also like to thank the people of Papua New Guinea whose help in my research on Tok Pisin has enabled me to use only actual utterances as example sentences in this work.

2. Washabaugh (1975) makes a similar claim in his paper on the development of the *fi* complementizer from a preposition in Providence Island Creole in Colombia. "The development of complementizers . . . is not a unique process for each distinct language, but rather this development in creolization, and perhaps in all cases of grammar elaboration, proceeds generally along the same route."

3. Whether or not a stable pidgin is created before creolization begins is determined by the social context. In a situation in which speakers from many linguistic groups are

mixed together and cut off from contact with their home groups, but not immersed in any new language, creolization begins immediately. This was the case with slaves in English and French colonies in the Caribbean. In a situation such as that found in Papua New Guinea in which speakers of many languages come into contact with each other but are not cut off from their home groups for any great length of time, a stable pidgin is likely to form. A forthcoming volume of papers on this subject, edited by William Washabaugh and myself, will be entitled *The Social Context of Creolization.*

4. If Tok Pisin had movement rules, it would probably be easier to distinguish between the preposition *long* and the complementizer *long.* For example, in ongoing work on Sranan Tongo, Jan Voorhoeve has had some success in distinguishing verbs from prepositions in a similar situation of syntactic reanalysis due to the fact that prepositions are fronted with the rest of the phrase whereas verbs remain behind.

5. This model of lexical subcategorization for complement type owes much to Grimshaw's (1979) account of lexical subcategorization for complement type in English, although the Tok Pisin system is much different than the English one.

6. One old woman about fifty years old from Manus did not fit this pattern at all. There were five instances of the verb *inap* plus a complement clause in her speech sample, and none of them were marked with *long.* It is likely that she speaks an even earlier dialect in which *inap* is subcategorized to take only bare S complements. See the discussion regarding Table 3.

7. All these speakers were born in rural villages, and all of them now live in urban areas, except for K. and P. who live in semi-urban areas. If there is a rural-urban continuum that parallels the age correlation with *long* deletion frequencies, this would explain why K. and P. are a bit conservative for their age groups regarding *long* deletion.

8. The frequency counts for *long* in the environment $[laik\_\_\_S]$ referred to here are as follows:

1943 data	1/50
1975 data	0/126

The single instance of *long* in this environment in the 1943 data is considered to be an error.

9. An overall comparison of the frequency of *long* versus $\emptyset$ in the environment $[VP\_\_\_S]$ in the data from Hall (1943) and my recent (1975) data also supports the claim that bare S complements are being replaced by more complex complements:

1943 data	4/65 (6%)
1975 data	55/141 (39%)

Of course the percentage in the 1975 data would be much higher if it were not for the COMP deletion rule that is now operating. In addition, this table does not reflect the fact that the use of embedded sentences is increasing as well.

10. This use of *olsem* is very similar to the use of *like* in the current dialect of English heard especially in California. Both are used as hesitation fillers and as a means of putting distance between the speaker and his statements. In this example, the speaker is trying to be polite while questioning the ridiculous statement that a Papua New Guinean army platoon was starving in the forest because their rations were late in arriving.

11. Most Tok Pisin speakers optionally bracket relative clauses with the *ia* marker at one or both ends of the clause, as described in Sankoff and Brown 1976.

12. I want to thank Ken Hale and John McCarthy for supplying this information about Irish and Biblical Hebrew.

13. In (35), an independently motivated rule of free pronoun deletion has deleted the resumptive pronoun in the relative clause as well as the object pronoun in the main clause.

ON THE SOCIALITY OF CREOLE LANGUAGES
William Washabaugh

Innate Blueprints

For some years now Derek Bickerton has been issuing a clarion call for a return to an autonomous linguistics, a linguistics independent of sociology. He has presented unambiguous statements like: "The creole continuum is first and foremost a LINGUISTIC and not a SOCIAL phenomenon" and "At the level of *parole,* social forces do have an effect on language; at the level of *langue* they hardly ever do" (Bickerton 1979:13f.); "The kind of blueprint that we have wired into our heads is not a blueprint which defines language negatively in terms of formal universals, but rather one that defines language positively . . . people already have a first language" (p. 15 of this volume). All these statements leave no doubt as to Bickerton's position which is that, in both creolization and decreolization, the brain is running the show. These linguistic processes either flow directly from, or are guided by, universal cerebral blueprints for language acquisition. These processes are cerebral from the first and then social only after the fact and in a trivial sense: "Once they HAVE happened, a kind of post-hoc folk linguistics swings into action, and social values are assigned to various forms and structures irrespective of what kind of linguistic change brought these forms and structures to birth." In Bickerton's program, the brain is the mother who gives birth to language, whereas society is the father who just stands by and waits for his chance to smile or frown on the product of the mother's efforts.

The results of Bickerton's program have certainly advanced our understanding of creole languages by giant steps. His program is exciting, and that excitement is due in large part to its simplicity. However, I will show here that Bickerton's simple program is, when scrutinized, simplistic, and that the excitement which it engenders is, in part, euphoric. My argument is divided into two parts: first, I will lay bare the intellectual roots of Bickerton's program, and I will show that these roots are neither thick nor deep; second, I will examine certain creole phenomena which I believe raise doubts about the empirical adequacy of Bickerton's cerebral linguistics.

On the Sociality of Language

Bickerton's terminology (e.g., *faculté de langage, langue, parole*) reflects a certain commitment to a Saussurean paradigm[1]—not to say that he is in agreement with the linguistic program outlined in the *Cours de Linguistique Générale* (CLG), but only that he is committed to some major principles of linguistic analysis which date to that seminal work. It would be correct enough to say that he is one of a school of linguists who are out to refine and clarify the contributions of Saussure and to rectify the inadequacies of Saussurean linguistics.

But with painful regularity disciples, who struggle to clarify and rectify a master's model, purge from that model subtleties which, in the first formulation, may appear as ambiguities or contradictions. Bickerton's program, along with the bulk of contemporary linguistic orthodoxy, seems to have fallen into this trap. Specifically, the clarity and power of Bickerton's program suggest that, while smelting the ore, he has lost some of the iron of Saussure's linguistics.

I will first assay the raw Saussurean model and then follow that model through its post-Saussurean transformation in which it gained power and simplicity but lost subtlety. The objective of this presentation is to recover the valuable ideas which were relegated to the slag pile during the post-Saussurean transformation, and to recycle them toward a subtler linguistics.

Saussure, with his head twisted back toward the 19th century, was smitten by three major views on language. First, there was neogrammarian universalism to which he had made no small contribution himself. According to that view, language is a collection of units of speech which result from universal, involuntary mechanical laws. Second, he was impressed by the sociologism of W. D. Whitney whose work was set squarely against the view that language is a natural organism regulated totally by involuntary laws. For Whitney, language is an institution arrived at through social interaction and convention. Third, Saussure was certainly subject to the psychologism which was in the air at the end of the 19th century (Hughes 1961)—not the mechanistic psychologism which surfaces in H. Paul's *Principles,* but a phenomenological psychology such as that born of Rickert and Dilthey.

Saussure twisted and turned his program of linguistics to try to bring these three major views into line. By 1894, his program had a shape. He saw that the regularities uncovered by the neogrammarians were not so much regularities of physical events, but of psychological states, *états de conscience* (Saussure 1974:24, 40). Accordingly, he divided linguistics into two sciences—one of which addressed empirical events, and the other of which, statics, addressed psychological states.

Saussure argued that linguistic statics was a branch of the more general study of human symboling. Yet he was not so concerned with the psychology of symbol production as with the relations between symbols, and relations between symbols in Saussure's view were products of social conventions (Whitney's sociologism is apparent here). This, the foundation of his program, is apparent in Saussure's notes of 1894.

But for the rest of his life, Saussure struggled with, and cannot be said to have solved, the question of the relative contribution of the individual and the society to language states. His concepts of *la langue* and *la parole* reflect the struggle. In his first course in general linguistics (1906) Saussure maintained that *la langue* was an individual fact and that *la parole* was the social fact of language. All that enters *la langue* must arrive from the social sphere of *la parole* where linguistic elements are "consecrated through use." In his second course (1908) he turned about and argued that *la langue*, being the product of the social consecration, was a social fact. *La parole* was the individual's realization of *la langue* as well as the game field in which individual variants vied for admission to *la langue*. In this second course, *la faculté du langue* was introduced, but never developed, and was described as the psychological potential extant in every individual to acquire *la langue*. It is a universal psychological condition, not a linguistic fact; it is a condition necessary for the social institution of language. In the CLG, the relations between *la langue, la parole,* and *la faculté* are left unresolved, though they are cosmetically resurfaced to give the appearance of consistency. Still, the principle remains that "there is nothing in *la langue* which has not entered through *la parole.*"

It should be apparent that the CLG is an unfinished work (Koerner 1973: 327). It offered a crooked path which had to be straightened by Saussure's followers. And one of the most confusing of its confusions was certainly the distinction between the psychological and the social in *la parole* and *la langue.*

The post-Saussurean resolution of this confusion between the psychological and the social marks the birth of European structuralism, a birth foreshadowed in, but only adumbrated by, the embryonic CLG. And for our purposes, it should be noted that the delivery of structuralism from the embryonic CLG would have been impossible without a stiff injection of Husserlian phenomenology which had the effect of spotlighting the psychological while soft-pedaling the social.

The structural trend in general linguistics which took root with the International Congresses of the late twenties and early thirties is now being reproved for its supposed estrangement from philosophy, whereas in reality the international protagonists of this movement had close and effective connections with phenomenology in its Husserlian and Hegelian versions (Jakobson 1970: 13).

The precise nature of the contribution of phenomenology to European structuralism is not so mysterious. That contribution is the notion of the "transcendental ego," the Husserlian subject, the view that the structure of knowledge, including linguistic knowledge, derives from the very faculties of the knower. Husserl's project "assumes that language is one of the objects supremely constituted by consciousness and that actual languages are very special cases of a possible language which consciousness holds the key to" (Merleau-Ponty 1964:84). The cerebralism, universalism, and mechanism of European structuralisms derive, in large part, from Husserl's notion of the consciousness of the subject.

A similar program—one founded on the same notion of "transcendental ego"—when tendered by Chomsky, exploded American linguistics which had not been primed by the philosophical inquiry that had always accompanied European linguistics.

Chomsky developed a notion which follows very closely the idea of the subject in Husserlian phenomenology. His explicit reference to this subject is symptomatic of the fact that Husserlian philosophy has been at the basis of signification theories in this century, and, consciously or not, explicitly or not, at the basis of modern linguistics (Coward and Ellis 1977:129).

We look upon generative linguistics as "Chomsky's Revolution," but it is in reality Chomsky's continuation of the structuralist revolution.

Bickerton is heir to this principle of the centrality and transcendentality of the ego, and to the view that language is an object which is constituted prior to experience. His understanding of *la langue* and *la faculté* parallels with unnerving consistency the Husserlian project described above (Bickerton 1975:179). In fact, he is a good deal more consistent in his commitment to this principle than other linguists who work within the generative linguistic program. Specifically, he is critical of "correlational sociolinguists" who advocate the generative program but whose methods run contrary to the phenomenological principles of that program. He argues that "choice of style is governed, not by any inter-subjective and objectively perceptible features in the situational context, but by the autonomous and fluctuating feelings of the speaker" (Bickerton 1975:184). "Thus, as with most linguistic phenomena of any interest, switching turns out to be an internal rather than an external process—to have its locus, not in society, but in the mind" (Bickerton 1977a:16).

The cerebralism which surfaces so regularly in Bickerton's linguistics is not a quirk, a whim, or a fetish. His "brainstorming" is not at all a carking after an unrealistic theoretical goal. Rather his cerebralism is well-measured; it is built upon no small linguistic and philosophical foundation. His program is nothing less than the continuation of the structuralist revolution and the transformation of contemporary linguistic theory into one which is consistent through and through with the fundamental phenomenological principle of the "transcendental ego."

Bickerton seems to be a Copernicus (Bickerton 1975) trying to convince the skeptics that the ego, like the sun, is not determined, but is central and determining. However, whereas the Copernican revolution won the day, the structuralist revolution falters even at its inception. Husserl backed off from his pure phenomenology (Roche 1973), and the European structuralists have now set for themselves the goal of de-constructing the ego.

> In this development, a Cartesian grammar would become redundant and linguistics would have to orient itself to a different view of the subject, one in which the subject is destroyed and re-made in the signifier—a theory which, as we have seen already, both Marxism and psychoanalysis would favor (Coward and Ellis 1977:130).

So instead of being a Copernican prophet who is discovering a revolutionary path toward a new understanding of the linguistic cosmos, Bickerton may be one of a crew of linguists which is now straightening and extending the path which the structuralist pioneers charted with the aid of their Husserlian compasses. Only that crew has not yet realized that the pioneers got lost in the woods.

Creole Language Change and the Sociality of Language

This is not the occasion on which to offer an alternative to the whole structuralist, cerebralist program. Instead I would like to get creole language studies "out of the woods" by returning to the subtle embryonic structuralism of Saussure and by rediscovering there principles for calming the current "brainstorms." Specifically, I will return to a program based on Saussure's seminal observation that *la langue* is a social fact.[2] I will apply this dictum—that language is a social fact—to creole phenomena which Bickerton would explain by appealing to the notion of innate blueprint. My purpose is to demonstrate that alternative explanations are available for these creole language phenomena which on first glance seem apt for his universalist explanation.

The phenomena to be presented here are not facts about creolization—the genesis of a creole language. Rather they are facts about changes that appear in creoles consequent to their genesis. Some such changes—namely, those which occur by borrowing—will be set to one side here. These changes by borrowing for which an explicit model or target exists will not be discussed. Instead we will consider internally motivated changes which are not modeled on an explicit target language.

In Bickerton's view (1979) such internally motivated changes are directed by an innate blueprint, the same innate blueprint which guides creolization. Just as creolization wherein "the child . . . has to make up the deficit [of an absent model], so the child has recourse to things which are somehow already in its knowledge" (p. 13 of this volume), so, too, in internally motivated changes the guidance system is cerebral, not social. The speaker is guided in his changes by things which are somehow already in his knowledge. It is as if internally motivated change were an ineluctable juggernaut which forces its way into *la langue* regardless of the extra-cerebral conditions of the speaker.

Bickerton does not refer to such change as a juggernaut, but such a word does not exaggerate his view. He argues, for example, that the vowel denasalization change which, as I reported (1978), accounts for the *mē-me* variation in the past tense marker of Providence Island Creole (PIC) is altogether cerebrally initiated and promoted. "The change came about through a regular phonological process, and the result HAD to be socially classified somehow" (Bickerton 1979:14). Bickerton's own emphatic use of HAD implies that the change which is to be classified has all the force of a linguistic juggernaut.

My objective here will be to demonstrate that the maintenance of this and of other internally motivated changes in PIC is a social rather than a cerebral affair, and that such changes might not be maintained if that selfsame PIC were displaced into different social settings—indeed, the *mē-me* variation is evidently not realized in many similar varieties of Caribbean English Creole (CEC). That objective will be achieved by showing that not only the *mē-me* variation but also at least four other innovations are curiously collocated in PIC. Whereas linguistic conditions in other varieties of CEC are enough like those of PIC to support all these same innovations, no other variety finds them so far advanced. My conclusion will be that these innovations perform a special social function for the people of Providence Island.

First, there is the *men fi* innovation. By this innovation PIC speakers subtly intensify the impact of a sentence by adding modal force. In (1) the placement of *men* before *fi* says that indeed the rock was intentionally tied on to hit the baby. The *fi* in the *men fi* construction is a complementizer which is governed by a deleted modal verb marked for past tense. The past tense marker *men* is made to carry the modal force of that deleted verb. Bickerton (1979) disagrees with this description,[3] but he does not disagree with the fact that this construction is rather rare in varieties of CEC. That last fact, on which there is agreement, is a crucial fact and one which is not accounted for by an innate blueprint.

(1) *Im tai a rak men fi go lik dong bis biebi.*
     He tied a rock to go hit down this baby.

A second innovation pertains to the directional complementizer *go* which occurs with verbs of motion in Caribbean English Creole (CEC) (2). My argument (Washabaugh forthcoming) is that this directional complementizer derives, through reanalysis, from the motion verb used in a serial verb construction. Some varieties of CEC have extended the reanalysis process from *go* to *kom* and *gan* (3), and have bleached the resulting complementizer of all features of directionality (4). This reanalysis process spreads to *kom* and *gan* in a pattern which bespeaks guidance by a cerebral gyroscope. But again, the furthest reaches of the extension of the innovation are found in PIC, and that fact will not be attributable to the brain.

(2) *She wash aut di swet an pres it an keri go gi im* (PIC).
     She washes out the sweat and presses it and carries it to give it to him.
(3) a. *Firs ting im go go pap af i haan bogota* (PIC).
        The first thing you know he will go break his arm in Bogota.
     b. *Dem kom ko saach mi hier* (PIC).
        They came to search my hair.
     c. *Dem ah gan ga tiif aut presh pinuts bota* (PIC).
        Then I went to steal P's peanut butter.
(4) *Ai mos kom aut go luk waif* (PIC).
     I must come out to look for a wife.

A third innovation has to do with the sentence-initial interrogative tag in CEC (5a). Roberts (1977) argues that such a tag is a recent spontaneous development in JC. I (Washabaugh 1977) showed this "spontaneous development account" to be false by presenting evidence for the existence of a lexically distinct but syntactically identical tag in PIC (5b). I can conceive of two alternatives to the "spontaneous development account," namely, a "survival account" and a "natural change account." The evidence for such a "survival account" is twofold. First, sentence-initial interrogative tags are quite infrequent in languages of the world. Second, the West African languages, Fante and Mandinka, are two among the handful of languages in which sentence-initial interrogative tags appear.

(5)   a. *Duont a tuu poliis faada ya av?*
         You have two fathers who are policemen, don't you?
      b. *Ent mi ponkin vain da gro?*
         My pumpkin vine is growing, right?

One might argue for a "natural change account" as an alternative to both the "spontaneous development account" and the "survival account." Evidence supporting the "natural change account" is two-fold. First, Roberts observed that the higher frequency of sentence-initial tag use appeared among children. Children are typically the purveyors of natural changes in languages. Second, I have recently observed frequent and regular use of sentence-initial tags in the speech of four-year-old American children (6) despite the fact that such utterances are unacceptable to most adult speakers of English. Such sentences support the "natural change account" since natural change is hypothesized to correspond inversely to the directionality of child language acquisition.

(6)   Right mosquitoes can't eat up clothes?

If the weight of further evidence should tip the scales toward a "natural change account" of interrogative tags, then again we would be confronted with a situation in which the creole speakers are promoting an innovation which leads their language away from both the historical basilect and the acrolect. And again, PIC is one of the few varieties of CEC in which this innovation has been observed.

A final innovation is the development of an iterative aspect marker in PIC. Whereas Bickerton (1976, 1977b) has argued that the iterative aspect is marked in all creole varieties, D. Taylor (1977:179) has shown that JC and Haitian Creole are exceptions. Like JC, basilectal PIC conveys iterative aspect with an unmarked verb. Whereas this gap in the evidence for Bickerton's hypothetical universals is problematic in its own right, it is not the focal point of the discussion here. The lack of a marker of the iterative in PIC is merely the stage on which the focal innovation plays itself out.

The innovation itself involves the reanalysis of the adjective *stodi (stodi-sodi-todi)* to serve as a marker of the iterative aspect as in (7). When so used, *stodi* combines with an unmarked verb and is never found in combination with another aspect marker. To add to the complexity of the description, I should note the existence of sentences (8a) and (8b) in which the adverbs *kiip* and *pyur* are used to mark iterativity. But in most instances these adverbs combine with the aspect marker *de* which regularly marks the continuative aspect.

(7) a. *Him stodi rait pan piepa an gi wi* (PIC).
     He is always writing on paper and giving it to us.
   b. *Di kau stodi mek im iirz go so.*
     The cow is always making his ears go so.
   c. *E. stodi bring mango fi dem.*
     E. always brings mango for them.
(8) a. *Ah kiip de bai saks.*
     I am always buying socks.
   b. *Im pyur de ron baut.*
     He is just running about.

A plausible explanation based on the facts presented above is that *stodi* is the first or earliest marker of iterativity in PIC. The variable appearance of *kiip* and *pyur* with *de* indicates that, through decreolization, the iterative aspect is occasionally signaled by the marker *de* rather than by *stodi*. Since the iterative *de* is not distinct from the continuative *de*, the adverbs *kiip* and *pyur* are combined with just the iterative *de*. As a later development, the iterative *de* may be deleted leaving only the appended adverbs *pyur* or *kiip* to mark iterativity.

The central feature of the innovation is that an iterative aspect marker *stodi* is developed in PIC at some point later than the creolization process. This development of the iterative aspect marker is a natural change, since it proceeds by a reanalysis of a formative which already exists in the language. And here again, the innovation occurs in PIC though not in other varieties of CEC, at least not in the same way. (Such an innovative use of *todi* is not mentioned by LePage and Cassidy [1967:446]; though see Baugh [1976] for a discussion of *steady* in BE.)

All these innovations are natural changes. In each, the innovative variants pop out of the language universal *faculté,* and each variant is built into the grammar gradually under the guidance of the cerebral gyroscope. But whereas these innovations may be natural, they are not inevitable. Their progress is not ineluctable. One single observation will make this clear. Bailey (1973:67) has argued that natural changes spread in waves; innovations move outward from a central point. The lects at the epicenter of a series of innovations will contain the most recent changes; lects most peripheral to the center of change will contain the fewest innovations. Such a principle would lead us to place PIC, replete as it is with innovations, at the epicenter of natural changes in CEC. But that seems most unlikely since, as we will note below, Providence Island is among the youngest and most isolated of CEC communities.

My argument is that despite their cerebral provenance, natural changes are maintained only if "consecrated by use." Like so many seeds which have fallen to the ground, these innovations will sprout of their own nature. But they will only take root when conditions are right. Each innovation has undoubtedly sprouted in other, maybe all, varieties of CEC. But the question remains, why have they not taken root everywhere? Or again, why have they taken root so tenaciously in PIC? The cerebral linguist is at a loss to answer these questions. But a sociologist will point out some facts about Providence Island which, although independent of the foregoing linguistic observations, coincide with them more neatly than chance would have it.

A first fact: The foundation of the Providence Island community was laid according to the basic West Indian blueprint. There were the well-moneyed and landed British who set the limits within which the black slaves could function (Mintz and Price 1976). But because of the geographical isolation of the island, the ties of the landowners to Britain, characteristically strong in other British West Indian communities (Mintz 1971), were weakened. Accordingly, the Providence Island British could not rejuvenate their social and cultural commitments, not to mention their political and economic relationships, to the motherland. The British influence, the British model, the British goal for social mobility were all drastically attenuated by the simple fact of geographical isolation.

A second fact: The Providence Island community since its founding has been held in the political pocket of Colombia. The last 150 years of its history witness unbroken Colombian hegemony in Providence Island, and that has to be significant given that the community is only about 190 years old.

A third fact: The island has spent most of its last 150 years in cultural limbo. The Colombians governed it but did not, until recently, follow up that governance with social interventions in island affairs. The reason for that is clear enough. Providence Island is just as geographically removed from Colombia as it is from the other West Indian communities.

These three facts, when taken together, create the image of a people who are British enough to know that they do not want to be identified with Africans (Price 1970), and who are free enough from Colombia not to be immediately hispanicized. But they are isolated enough from everyone that all their social and linguistic models and targets are fuzzy. The islanders' response to this situation is ambivalent. One the one hand, they are moving toward the weak and fuzzy model supplied by the British and, more recently, by American language and culture. This movement surfaces as decreolization. But, on the other hand, they are moving toward a distinctive identity which is neither American nor African. The collocation of unusual linguistic innovations in PIC symbolizes that distinctive identity. Their "innovated" language shows the people of Providence Island "that they belong to a place" (LePage 1977:110) which is neither an acrolectal "place" nor a basilectal "place," neither a "place" with the Anglo, nor a "place" with the African. Their "innovated" language shows the people of Providence Island that they belong to a distinct "place" and that they have a distinct identity.

Such a movement could be unusually strong in Providence Island where there are not such clear economic and political benefits to be derived from assimilating to the Anglo model as in other West Indian communities. The sense of unity and equality of all islanders (Wilson 1973:44ff.) is stronger in this community which is not clearly divided by class lines (Davenport 1961). So, the pressure to establish markers of their identity and their unity is strong in Providence Island, and that pressure fertilizes the ground in which innovations sprout. The maintenance of these natural changes in Providence Island is a product, not of cerebral forces, but of a suitable social situation for the nurturing of innovations.

With this analysis I am not impugning Bickerton's distinction between natural change and decreolization. It is certainly helpful to see how innovations originate. But I am arguing that he has carried the distinction too far by arguing that "natural change" proceeds without influence from social factors. My argument is that no innovation is maintained in a language without some pressure from factors external to the brain.

NOTES

1. I am aware of the controversy which has been engendered by Koerner's talk (1972) of a Saussurean-Chomskyan paradigm. But I doubt that my adoption of Koerner's notion for rhetorical and heuristic purposes affects the substance of my argument. The historiographical analysis outlined here is more fully explicated in Washabaugh (1974; 1976).

2. As I have indicated in Washabaugh (1976), Saussure's notion of the sociality of language is irremediably flawed. Specifically, the idea that the sociality of *la langue* consists in its distribution to each member of the language community is an overly mechanical concept of sociality. So when I suggest that we must return to Saussure's seminal observation that *la langue* is a social fact, I mean only that we must return to the spirit of that observation, not to its substance.

3. Bickerton argues that sentence (1) contains an embedded sentence whose verb *go* is combined with the modal auxiliary *fi* and which is marked for anterior aspect by *men*. I, on the other hand, have argued that *fi* in (1) is an infinitive marker bearing the force of a deleted verb which is marked for past tense (or anterior aspect).

Bickerton argues against my analysis by citing evidence to show that nonfinite sentences do not exist in contemporary CEC basilects. Another way of stating this same claim is to say that CEC basilects lack a raising transformation which would move a subject out of an embedded clause leaving the verb subjectless or nonfinite. But I have strong doubts about this claim.

My doubts should not be misconstrued as the obverse of a belief that all *fi*'s, aside from *fi* prepositions, are infinitive markers. I do not subscribe to such a claim. In fact, I have argued at length (Washabaugh 1975) that in historical basilects of CEC, now irrecoverably eroded, *fi* was not an infinitive marker. I argued, using sentences like (9), that *fi* is a complementizer which marks a sentence from which the subject has not been raised. My argument is that (9) is a sentence in which the *fi* complementizer marks an embedded finite sentence.

(9)   *Ah waan di rien kom fi ah don go huoam* (PIC).
      I want the rain to come so that I won't have to go home.

Sentences like (9) are rare in most contemporary varieties of CEC, but they are frequent enough in older texts. The frequency of sentences like (9) in older texts warrants the claim that the *fi* infinitive marker, which is so prevalent in all varieties of CEC, derives from the *fi* which in the past marked embedded finite verbs. That latter *fi* in turn is derived from a preposition. In sentences like (9), *fi* is a complementizer, the use of which does not imply the application of a raising transformation. All other uses of the *fi* complementizer of which I am aware do imply an application of a raising transformation.

That having been said, let us consider Bickerton's argument that raising does not apply in other types of *fi* sentences in CEC basilects. First, he presents the sentence (10) (see his p. 8) to demonstrate that the pronoun of an embedded sentence could not have been raised. By observing that the presence of the pronoun *am* renders sentence (10) ungrammatical, Bickerton concludes that subject to object (S-O) raising cannot apply in GC. One might extend this same sort of argument to the French sentence *je crois qu'il est riche,* and one might conclude that because **je le crois etre riche* is ungrammatical, that French lacks S-O raising. But such an argument would overlook the acceptability of *je le crois riche* which indicates that raising applies in French under certain conditions which need not be specified in English (Eckman 1975). Bickerton's sentence (10b) seems to be ungrammatical for just the same sort of reason—that is, (10b) is ungrammatical not because (S-O) raising is unavailable in GC, but because the raising of *am* without deletion of the aspect marker *a* violates the universal "specified subject constraint."

(10) a. *Mi sii i a kom.*
         I saw him coming.
      b. **Mi sii am a kom.*
(11) *Mi sii im kom.*
      I saw him coming.

Second, Bickerton has tried to maintain his claim that raising cannot apply in CEC by parrying my argument that the applicability of S-S raising in CEC, as in (12), implies the applicability of S-O raising (Eckman 1975). Bickerton (1977c:355) replies to this argument that S-S may apply at the mesolectal level and still be inapplicable at the basilectal level. And so, by reason of the variability in the creole continuum, the implicational relationship between S-S and S-O raising does not hold. My rebuttal to Bickerton's reply is that whereas the implicational relationship may not hold for the creole continuum, it should hold for individuals within the continuum. So, for example, sentence (13) is produced by Miss Kate, an 80-year-old Bottomhouse woman, whose speech I would impressionistically classify as basilectal. But Miss Kate also produced sentence (12), and regularly produces such sentences, in which S-S raising has been applied. Now if Miss Kate has acquired an ability to apply S-S raising systematically, she should, by implication, also have an ability to apply S-O raising. I suggest that sentence (13) is just such an example of a sentence in which S-O raising has been applied.

(12) *I (gras) haad fi ded.*
      That grass doesn't die easily.
(13) *Ai ekspek me fi go tu mista R. haus yeside.*
      I expected to go to Mr. R.'s house yesterday.

But perhaps Bickerton would want to argue that even if Miss Kate could apply both S-O and S-S raising, sentence (13) is not a sentence in which either raising has been applied. Perhaps he would want to argue that whereas *fi* in some sentences is reanalyzed as a complementizer, the *fi* in sentences like (13) is still a verb. Such a situation of incomplete reanalysis of a formative is not unknown for creoles (Roberts 1975).

However, such a suggestion would be most unlikely unless Bickerton would be willing to argue that some *fi*'s, and their *to* reflexes, are never reanalyzed within the creole continuum. For it is a fact that sentences like (14) appear everywhere in the Providence Island continuum through to the acrolect. In such sentences the *men* and *fi* are replaced by *waz* and *tu,* but the sentences nevertheless exhibit the same structural arrangement of formatives as those of (13) and (8). Unless Bickerton is willing to argue that *tu* in the sentences (14a) and (14b) is a verb, then his argument will founder on those sentences. My description of the structure of (8) is that it contains an infinitive marker *fi*; I would carry over that same argument and apply it to (14), saying that *tu* in these sentences is an infinitive marker.

(14)   a.   *I told you was to invite Bill.*
       b.   *You promise was to sell me some coconut.*

I will admit that the variability of structures in the creole continuum places formidable methodological obstacles in the way of cogent syntactic argumentation. So formidable are they that Bickerton's own arguments against the applicability of S-O raising in CEC occasionally trip over them. Bickerton argues that the pronoun in sentence (9) above is not raised out of the embedded sentence. (He argues this despite the fact that this is a sentence which I already grant that raising does not apply to.) But his argument against raising is based on the fact that the pronoun following *fi* exhibits a subjective rather than an objective form. This is the weakest of his arguments, for Bickerton should recognize that the form of a pronoun in PIC is highly variable and certainly subject to some hypercorrection. So at the basilect level there is no *ah/mi* pronominal distinction, as in sentence (15); at another level of the continuum the use of *ah* may be overgeneralized as in the nearly acrolectal (16). Sentence (16), along with the collection of sentences like (9) which appears in Washabaugh (1975:118), should be sufficient to illustrate that the forms of pronouns in PIC are highly variable and will not provide any firm foundation for a syntactic argument.

(15)   *Di bwai kos mi se mi krebm.*
       The boy cussed me saying that I am craven.
(16)   *Yu gaiz nat fier. Un wudn let ai vuoat.*
       You guys are not fair. You wouldn't let me vote.

On a number of counts then, Bickerton's case against raising in CEC is weak. First, his evidence for the inapplicabilty of raising in GC is too restricted. Second, his argument that the variability of the creole continuum nullifies the implicational relationship between S-S and S-O raising founders on the observation that both types of raising are applied by a single individual who frequently uses the *men fi* construction. Third, his argument that *fi* in CEC undergoes reanalysis from a verb to an infinitive marker, and that, as reanalysis proceeds, the *men fi* construction is lost, fails to account for the existence of the structurally similar *waz tu* construction throughout the creole continuum.

My analysis of the *men fi* construction avoids, on the one hand, all these difficulties, and yet it accords, on the other hand, with a variety of facts besides those which directly motivate it. First, my analysis accounts as neatly as Bickerton's for the fact that the *men fi* construction never occurs without the application of EQUI deletion to the clause marked by *fi*. Let me demonstrate the argument with sentence (17). Bickerton's hypothetical sentence (17a) is ungrammatical because such a sentence would have to be derived from something like (yong mahn past-se)$_{S3}$(mi past-oblige)$_{S2}$(fi me past-tel yu)$_{S1}$. But such an underlying string could never be generated because of a selection restriction on *oblige* which requires that its subject and the subject of the clause which it dominates be identical (Perlmutter 1971:9f.). Note, however, that a sentence like (17b) is grammatical because it is derived from (yong mahn past-se)$_{S3}$(mi past-oblige)$_{S2}$ (fi me past-tel yu)$_{S1}$ which does not violate such a selectional restriction. The postulation of an underlying abstract verb *oblige* was independently motivated in Washabaugh (1975). The task of accounting for the ungrammaticality of (17a) follows straightforwardly from that argument and observes that if the verb dominating *fi* is *oblige,* then the subject of the clause dominated by *oblige* will always be subject to EQUI deletion because of the "like subjects constraint" attached to *oblige.*

(17)   a.   *Yong mahn se men fi mi tel yu se mis missi ded.*
       b.   *Yong mahn se mi men fi tel yu se mis missi ded.*
            The young man said that I should tell you that Miss Missi is dead.

Second, I claim that the *fi* infinitive marker in (8) exhibits a certain verbiness only because it shares the force of a deleted verb. This claim accords with Huddleston's (1971:295) analysis of *to* in English (18) which also has a certain verbiness about it. Huddleston argues that the *to* in (18) is an infinitive marker, and that the *are* is a modal auxiliary. Would Bickerton contravene that argument and say that for English (18), as he has for PIC (14), the *to* is a verb?

(18)   You're to leave immediately.

Finally, my claim that the *fi* complementizer in (8) derives historically from a preposition rather than from a verb squares with masses of evidence which have demonstrated affinities between complementizers and prepositions (Washabaugh 1975:134).

REFERENCES

Agheyisi, Rebecca. 1971. West African Pidgin: Simplification and Simplicity. Unpublished doctoral dissertation. Stanford University.

Allen, Cynthia. 1977. Topics in Diachronic English Syntax. Unpublished doctoral dissertation. University of Massachusetts, Amherst.

Alleyne, Mervyn. 1971. Acculturation and the Cultural Matrix of Creolization. In *Pidginization and Creolization of Languages*. Ed. by Dell Hymes, pp. 169-86. London: Cambridge University Press.

———. 1979. Opening Remarks. From the Conference on Theoretical Orientations in Creole Studies, March 28-April 1, 1979, St. Thomas, Virgin Islands.

Anderson, Roger. 1979. Creolization as the Acquisition of a Second Language as a First Language. From the Conference on Theoretical Orientations in Creole Studies, March 28-April 1, 1979, St. Thomas, Virgin Islands.

Bailey, Charles-James. 1973. *Variation and Linguistic Theory*. Arlington, VA: Center for Applied Linguistics.

Baugh, John. 1976. The State of 'steady': Aspectual Marking in Black English. MS. From the Annual Conference of the LSA, Philadelphia.

Benveniste, Emile. 1957. La phrase relative: problème de syntaxe générale. *Bulletin de la Société de Linguistique de Paris* 53.39-54.

Bever, T. G., and D. T. Langendoen. 1972. The Interaction of Speech Perception and Grammatical Structure in the Evolution of Language. In *Linguistic Change and Generative Theory*. Ed. by Robert Stockwell and K. S. Macaulay. Bloomington, IN: Indiana University Press.

Bickerton, Derek. 1973. The Nature of a Creole Continuum. *Language* 49.640-69.

———. 1974. Creolization, Linguistic Universals, Natural Semantax and the Brain. *University of Hawaii Working Papers in Linguistics* 6.3.124-41.

———. 1975. *Dynamics of a Creole System*. London and New York: Cambridge University Press.

———. 1976. Creole Tense-Aspect Systems and Universal Grammar. From the Society of Caribbean Linguistics Conference, Georgetown, Guyana.

———. 1977a. What Happens When We Switch. MS. Prepared for the Robert B. LePage Festschrift.

———. 1977b. Pidginization and Creolization: Language Acquisition and Language Universals. In *Pidgin and Creole Linguistics*. Ed. by Albert

Valdman, pp. 49-69. Bloomington, IN: Indiana University Press.

———. 1977c. Putting Back the Clock in Variation Studies. *Language* 53. 353-61.

———. 1979. Decreolization and the Creole Continuum. From the Conference on Theoretical Orientations in Creole Studies, March 28-April 1, 1979, St. Thomas, Virgin Islands.

Bickerton, Derek, and C. Odo. 1976. Change and Variation in Hawaiian English. Vol. 1. *General Phonology and Pidgin Syntax* (Final Report on NSF Project No. GS-39748).

Bourdieu, Pierre, and Luc Boltanski. 1975. Le fétichisme de la langue. *Actes de la Recherche en Sciences Sociales* 4.2-32.

Bradshaw, Joel. 1978. The Origins of Syntax in Syntax. From the 1978 Summer Meeting of the Linguistic Society of America.

Butterworth, G., and E. M. Hatch. 1978. A Spanish-Speaking Adolescent's Acquisition of English Syntax. In *Second Language Acquisition.* Ed. by E. M. Hatch, pp. 231-45. Rowley, MA: Newbury House Publishers.

Cazden, C. 1972. *Child Language and Education.* New York: Holt, Rinehart and Winston.

Clark, H., and E. Clark. 1977. *Psychology and Language.* New York: Harcourt Brace Jovanovich.

Clark, Ross. 1979. In Search of Beach-La-Mar: Towards a History of Pacific Pidgin English. Revised MS. Auckland.

Corder, S. P. 1967. The Significance of Learners' Errors. *International Review of Applied Linguistics* 5.161-70.

———. 1975. 'Simple Codes' and the Source of the Second Language Learner's Initial Heuristic Hypothesis. From the Colloque, 'Theoretical Models in Applied Linguistics' IV, Université de Neuchâtel.

Coward, Rosalind, and John Ellis. 1977. *Language and Materialism: Developments in Semiology and the Theory of the Subject.* Boston: Routledge and Kegan Paul.

Davenport, W. 1961. Introduction. *Social and Economic Studies* 10(4).

DeCamp, David. 1971a. Introduction: The Study of Pidgin and Creole Languages. In *Pidginization and Creolization of Languages.* Ed. by Dell Hymes, pp. 13-39. London: Cambridge University Press.

———. 1971b. Toward a Generative Analysis of a Post-Creole Speech Continuum. In *Pidginization and Creolization of Languages.* Ed. by Dell Hymes, pp. 349-70. London: Cambridge University Press.

Dutton, T. E. 1978. Tracing the Origin of Hiri (or Police) Motu—Issues and Problems. From the Second International Conference on Austronesian

Linguistics. Canberra: Australian National University Press.

Eckman, Fred. 1975. On Explaining Some Typological Facts about Raising. From the Annual Conference of the LSA, San Francisco.

Emonds, Joseph. 1976. *A Transformational Approach to English Syntax.* New York: Academic Press.

Ferguson, Charles A. 1977. Linguistic Theory. *Bilingual Education: Current Perspectives,* Vol. II Linguistics. Washington, DC: Center for Applied Linguistics.

Geraghty, Paul. 1978. Fijian Dialect Diversity and Foreigner Talk: The Evidence of Pre-Missionary Manuscripts. In *Fijian Language Studies: Borrowing and Pidginization.* Ed. by Albert J. Schütz, pp. 51-67. (Bulletin of the Fiji Museum, Vol. 4.)

Grimes, Joseph E. 1972. Outlines and Overlays. *Language* 48.513-24.

Grimshaw, Jane. 1979. Complement Selection and the Lexicon. *Linguistic Inquiry* 10.279-326.

Gumperz, John J. 1968. Types of Linguistic Communities. In *Readings in the Sociology of Language.* Ed. by Joshua A. Fishman, pp. 460-70. The Hague: Mouton.

Hall, Robert A., Jr. 1943. *Melanesian Pidgin English: Grammar, Texts, Vocabulary.* Baltimore: Linguistic Society of America.

———. 1962. The Life Cycle of Pidgin Languages. *Lingua* 11.151-56.

———. 1966. *Pidgin and Creole Languages.* Ithaca: Cornell University Press.

Halliday, M. A. K. 1975. Language as a Social Semiotic: Towards a General Sociolinguistic Theory. In *The First LACUS Forum 1974.* Ed. by Adam Makkai and Valerie Becker Makkai, pp. 17-46. Columbia, SC: Hornbeam Press.

Hatch, E. M. 1978. Discourse Analysis and Second Language Acquisition. In *Second Language Acquisition.* Ed. by E. M. Hatch, pp. 401-35. Rowley, MA: Newbury House Publishers.

Hatch, E. M., R. Shapira and J. Gough. 1978. "Foreigner-Talk" Discourse. I T L. *Review of Applied Linguistics* 39-40.39-60.

Huddleston, Rodney. 1971. *The Sentence in Written English.* New York: Cambridge University Press.

Hughes, H. Stuart. 1961. *Consciousness and Society: The Reorientation of European Thought 1890-1930.* New York: Knopf.

Hymes, Dell H. 1967. Models of the Interaction of Language and Social Setting. *Journal of Social Issues* 23.8-28.

Jakobson, Roman. 1970. *Main Trends in the Science of Language.* New York: Harper and Row.

Kennan, E. O. 1974. Conversational Competence in Children. *Journal of Child Language* 1-2.163-84.

Koerner, E. F. K. 1972. Towards a Historiography of Linguistics. *Anthropological Linguistics* 14.255-75.

———. 1973. *Ferdinand de Saussure: Origin and Development of His Linguistic Thought in Western Studies of Language.* Braunschweig: Vieweg.

Krashen, S. 1975. The Critical Period Hypothesis and Its Possible Bases. In *Developmental Psycholinguistics and Communication Disorders.* Ed. by D. R. Aaronson and R. W. Ricker. New York: The New York Academy of Sciences.

———. 1978. Adult Second Language Acquisition and Learning: A Review of Theory and Applications. In *Second Language Acquisition and Foreign Language Teaching.* Ed. by R. Gingras. Washington, DC: Center for Applied Linguistics.

Labov, William. 1972. The Internal Evolution of Linguistic Rules. In *Linguistic Change and Generative Theory.* Ed. by Robert Stockwell and K. S. Macaulay. Bloomington, IN: Indiana University Press.

Lambert, W. E. 1972. A Social Psychology of Bilingualism. In *Sociolinguistics.* Ed. by J. B. Pride and J. Holmes. Middlesex: Penguin.

Lamendella, J. T. 1977. General Principles of Neurofunctional Organization and Their Manifestation in Primary and Nonprimary Language Acquisition. *Language Learning* 27.155-96.

Langacker, Ronald. 1977. Syntactic Reanalysis. In *Mechanisms of Syntactic Change.* Ed. by C. Li. Austin: University of Texas Press.

Lazar-Meyn, Heidi. 1977. *Save* and *Stap* in Tok Pisin. *Penn Review of Linguistics* 2.2.23-32.

Lehmann, Winfred. 1972. Proto-Germanic Syntax. In *Toward a Grammar of Proto-Germanic.* Ed. by Frans van Coetsem and H. L. Kufner, pp. 239-68. Tübingen: Niemeyer.

LePage, Robert B. 1977. De-creolization and Re-creolization. *York Papers in Linguistics* 7.103-28.

LePage, Robert B., and F. Cassidy. 1967. *Dictionary of Jamaican English.* New York: Cambridge University Press.

Lord, Carol. 1976. Evidence for Syntactic Reanalysis: From Verb to Complementizer in Kwa. In *Papers from the Parasession on Diachronic Syntax.* Ed. by S. Steever et al. Chicago: Chicago Linguistic Society.

Merleau-Ponty, Maurice. 1964. *Signs.* Evanston: Northwestern University Press.

Mihalic, Francis. 1957. *Grammar and Dictionary of Neo-Melanesian.* Westmead, New South Wales, Australia: The Mission Press.

———. 1971. *The Jacaranda Dictionary and Grammar of Melanesian Pidgin.* Brisbane: Jacaranda Press.

Mintz, Sidney W. 1971. The Socio-Historical Background of Pidginization and Creolization. In *Pidginization and Creolization of Languages.* Ed. by Dell Hymes, pp. 481-96. London: Cambridge University Press.

Mintz, Sidney W., and R. Price. 1976. *An Anthropological Approach to the Afro-American Past: A Caribbean Perspective.* Philadelphia: Ishi.

Moag, Rodney F. 1973. A Phonological Grammar of Style Variation in Malayalam. Unpublished doctoral dissertation. University of Wisconsin.

———. 1977. *Fiji Hindi: A Basic Course and Reference Grammar.* Canberra: Australian National University Press.

———. 1978. Standardization in Pidgin Fijian: Implications for the Theory of Pidginization. In *Fijian Language Studies: Borrowing and Pidginization.* Ed. by Albert J. Schütz, pp. 68-90. (Bulletin of the Fiji Museum, Vol. 4.)

———. Forthcoming a. The Linguistic Adaptations of the Fiji Indians. In *Rama's Banishment: A Centenary Tribute to the Fiji Indians.* Ed. by Vijay C. Mishra. Auckland: Heinemann.

———. Forthcoming b. The Life Cycle of Non-Native Englishes: A Case Study of Fiji and the South Pacific. From the Conference on English in Non-Native Contexts, June 30-July 2, 1978, University of Illinois.

———. Forthcoming c. On the Correlation Between Language Situation and Socio-Economic Conditions. MS. May, 1979.

———. Forthcoming d. English as a Foreign, Second, Native, and Basal Language. From the Conference on English in Non-Native Contexts, June 30-July 2, 1978, University of Illinois.

Moag, Rodney F., and Louisa B. Moag. 1977. English in Fiji, Some Perspectives and the Need for Language Planning. *Fiji English Teachers Journal* 13.2-26.

Mühlhäusler, Peter. 1976a. Growth and Structure of the Lexicon of New Guinea Pidgin. Unpublished doctoral dissertation. Australian National University.

———. 1976b. The Category of Number in New Guinea Pidgin. *Linguistic Communications* 13.21-37.

———. 1979. Structural Expansion and the Process of Creolization. Position Papers, Part I, Conference on Theoretical Orientations in Creole Studies, March 28-April 1, 1979, St. Thomas, Virgin Islands, pp. 1-45.

———. Forthcoming. Complementation. In *Handbook of New Guinea Pidgin.* Ed. by Stephen A. Wurm. Canberra: Pacific Linguistics.

Naro, Anthony J. 1978. A Study on the Origins of Pidginization. *Language* 54.314-47.

Newport, E., H. Gleitman and L. Gleitman. 1977. Mother, I'd Rather Do It Myself: Some Effects and Non-Effects of Maternal Speech Style. In *Talking to Children*. Ed. by C. Snow and Charles A. Ferguson. New York: Cambridge University Press.

Perlmutter, David M. 1971. *Deep and Surface Structure Constraints in Syntax.* New York: Holt, Rinehart and Winston.

Platt, J. 1978. The Concept of a 'Creoloid': Exemplification: Basilectal Singapore English. In *Papers in Pidgin and Creole Linguistics*, No. 1. Ed. by L. Todd et al. Canberra: Australian National University Press.

Price, Thomas. 1970. Ethnohistory and Self-Image in Three New World Negro Societies. In *Afro-American Anthropology*. Ed. by N. Whitten and J. Szwed. New York: The Free Press.

Pride, John. 1978. Communicative Needs in the Learning and Use of English. From the East-West Center Conference on English as an International Auxiliary Language, March, 1978, Honolulu, Hawaii.

[Queensland.] 1885. Proceedings of the Legislative Assembly Session. Brisbane: Royal Commission on Recruiting Polynesian Labourers in New Guinea and Adjacent Islands.

Reinecke, John E. 1937. Marginal Languages: A Sociological Survey of the Creole Languages and Trade Jargons. Unpublished doctoral dissertation. Yale University.

———. 1938. Trade Jargons and Creole Dialects as Marginal Languages. *Social Forces* 17.107-18.

Roberts, Peter. 1975. The Adequacy of Certain Theories in Accounting for Important Grammatical Relationships in Creole Languages. From the International Conference on Pidgins and Creoles, Honolulu, Hawaii.

———. 1977. *Duont*: A Case for Spontaneous Development. *Journal of Creole Studies* 1.1.101-08.

Robson, B. 1975. On the Differences Between Creoles and Other Natural Languages. Mimeo.

Roche, Maurice. 1973. *Phenomenology, Language and the Social Sciences.* Boston: Routledge and Kegan Paul.

Rosansky, E. J. 1975. The Critical Period for the Acquisition of Language: Some Cognitive Developmental Considerations. *Working Papers in Bilingualism* 6.93-100.

Samarin, William. 1971. Salient and Substantive Pidginization. In *Pidginization and Creolization of Languages*. Ed. by Dell Hymes, pp. 117-40. London: Cambridge University Press.

Sankoff, Gillian. 1977a. Variability and Explanation in Language and Culture:

Cliticization in New Guinea Tok Pisin. In *Linguistics and Anthropology.* Ed. by M. Saville-Troike, pp. 59-73. Washington, DC: Georgetown University Press.

———. 1977b. Creolization and Syntactic Change in New Guinea Tok Pisin. In *Sociocultural Dimensions of Language Change.* Ed. by B. Blount and Mary Sanches, pp. 131-59. New York: Academic Press.

———. 1979a. Linguistic Variation in Pidgin-Creole Studies. From the Conference on Theoretical Orientations in Creole Studies, March 28-April 1, 1979, St. Thomas, Virgin Islands.

———. 1979b. The Genesis of a Language. (This volume.)

Sankoff, Gillian, and Penelope Brown. 1976. The Origin of Syntax in Discourse: A Case Study of Tok Pisin Relatives. *Language* 52.631-66.

Sankoff, Gillian, and Susan Laberge. 1973. On the Acquisition of Native Speakers by a Language. *Kivung* 6.32-47.

Saussure, Ferdinand de. 1974. *Notes Inédits sur Linguistique Générale. Fascicle 4 of Cours de Linguistique Générale, Edition Critique par R. Engler.* Wiesbaden: Harrassowitz.

Schiffrin, Deborah. 1976. A History of Determiners in Tok Pisin. Paper prepared for Linguistics 440. MS. 32 pp.

Schumann, J. H. 1978. The Acculturation Model for Second Language Acquisition. In *Second Language Acquisition and Foreign Language Teaching.* Ed. by R. Gingras. Washington, DC: Center for Applied Linguistics.

Scollon, R. T. 1974. One Child's Language from One to Two: The Origins of Construction. Unpublished doctoral dissertation. University of Hawaii.

Selinker, Larry. 1972. Interlanguage. *International Journal of Applied Linguistics* 10.209-31.
Also: *Error Analysis: Perspectives on Second Language Acquisition.* Ed. by Jack Richards, pp. 31-54. London: Longman Group Ltd., 1972.

Selinker, Larry, and J. T. Lamendella. 1978. Two Perspectives on Fossilization in Interlanguage Learning. *Interlanguage Studies Bulletin,* pp. 144-91.
Also: *Second Language Acquisition and Foreign Language Teaching.* Ed. by R. Gingras. Washington, DC: Center for Applied Linguistics, 1978.

Shipley, E., C. Smith and L. Gleitman. 1969. A Study in the Acquisition of Language: Free Responses to Commands. *Language* 45.322-42.

Slobin, D. I. 1973. Cognitive Prerequisites for the Development of Grammar. In *Studies of Child Language Development.* Ed. by Charles A. Ferguson and D. I. Slobin. New York: Holt, Rinehart and Winston.

Smith, D. M. 1973. Pidginization and Language Socialization: The Role of Marking. Unpublished MS. Georgetown University.

Snow, C., and Charles A. Ferguson, eds. 1977. *Talking to Children*. New York: Cambridge University Press.

Stauble, A. M. Forthcoming. Acculturation and Second Language Acquisition. In *Research in Second Language Acquisition*. Ed. by S. Krashen and R. Scarcella. Rowley, MA: Newbury House Publishers.

Taylor, A. 1978. Evidence of a Pidgin Motu in the Earliest Written Motu Materials. *Proceedings of the Second International Conference on Austronesian Linguistics*. Canberra: Australian National University Press.

Taylor, Douglas. 1977. *Languages of the West Indies*. Baltimore: Johns Hopkins University Press.

Todd, Loreto. 1974. *Pidgins and Creoles*. London: Routledge and Kegan Paul.

Traugott, Elizabeth. 1972. *A History of English Syntax*. New York: Holt, Rinehart and Winston.

Voorhoeve, Jan. 1971. Varieties of Creole in Suriname: Church Creole and Pagan Cult Languages. In *Pidginization and Creolization of Languages*. Ed. by Dell Hymes, pp. 305-15. London: Cambridge University Press.

Washabaugh, William. 1974. Saussure, Durkheim and Sociolinguistic Theory. *Archivum Linguisticum* 5.25-34.

–––. 1975. On the Development of Complementizers in Creolization. *Working Papers on Language Universals* 17.109-40.

–––. 1976. The History of Linguistics and the Theoretical Status of Inherent Variability. *Proceedings of the Mid-America Linguistics Conference*, pp. 515-54. Lawrence, KS: University of Kansas Press.

–––. 1977. A Note on 'duont'. Mimeo.

–––. 1978. Complexities in Creole Continua. *Lingua* 46.245-61.

–––. 1979. Brainstorming Creole Languages. From the Conference on Theoretical Orientations in Creole Studies, March 28-April 1, 1979, St. Thomas, Virgin Islands.

–––. Forthcoming. Pursuing Creole Roots. In *Generative Studies in Creole Languages*. Ed. by Pieter Muysken. Dordrecht: Foris.

Weinreich, Uriel, William Labov and Marvin Herzog. 1968. Empirical Foundations for a Theory of Language Change. In *Directions for Historical Linguistics: A Symposium*. Ed. by Winfred Lehmann and Yakov Malkiel, pp. 95-195. Austin: University of Texas Press.

Whinnom, Keith. 1965. The Origin of the European Based Creoles and Pidgins. *Orbis* 14.509-27.

Wilson, Peter. 1973. *Crab Antics*. New Haven: Yale University Press.

Woolford, Ellen. 1977. Aspects of Tok Pisin Grammar. Unpublished doctoral dissertation. Duke University.

———. 1978a. Topicalization and Clefting without *wh*-Movement. In *Proceedings of the Eighth Annual Meeting of the North Eastern Linguistic Society*. Ed. by Mark J. Stein. Amherst, MA.

———. 1978b. Free Relatives and Other Base Generated *wh*-Constructions. In *Papers from the Fourteenth Regional Meeting of the Chicago Linguistic Society*. Ed. by D. Farcas et al. Chicago: Chicago Linguistic Society.

———. Forthcoming. The Developing Complementizer System of Tok Pisin. In *Generative Studies in Creole Languages*. Ed. by Pieter Muyskcn. Dordrecht: Foris.

Wurm, Stephen A. 1971. New Guinea Highlands Pidgin: Course Materials. *Pacific Linguistics Series D*, No. 3.

Wurm, Stephen A. 1977. Pidgins, Creoles, Lingue Franche, and National Development. In *Pidgin and Creole Linguistics*. Ed. by Albert Valdman, pp. 333-57. Bloomington, IN: Indiana University Press.